ESSENTIAL PSYCHOLOGY

General Editor
Peter Herriot

F7

IMAGES OF MAN IN PSYCHOLOGICAL RESEARCH

ESSENTIAL

PSYCHOLOGY

IMAGES OF MAN IN PSYCHOLOGICAL RESEARCH

John Shotter

Methuen

First published 1975 by Methuen & Co Ltd
11 New Fetter Lane, London EC4P 4EE
© 1975 John Shotter
Printed in Great Britain by
Richard Clay (The Chaucer Press), Ltd
Bungay, Suffolk

ISBN (hardback) 0 416 81730 0
ISBN (paperback) 0 416 81740 8

We are grateful to Grant McIntyre of Open
Books Publishing Ltd for assistance in the
preparation of this series.

Contents

5

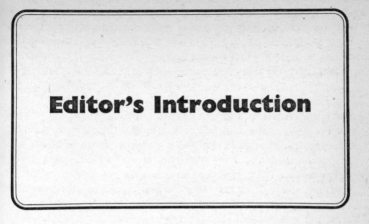

Editor's Introduction

John Shotter pleads for a change in the images of man which are implied by the ways in which we behave as psychologists. Our research and thinking has been dominated by views of man as an object, acted upon by forces outside his control. Shotter wishes us to consider man as an agent, and maintains that psychology should be a moral science of action.

Images of Man in Psychological Research belongs to Unit F of *Essential Psychology*. What unifies the books in this unit is the concept of change, not only in people but also in psychology. Both the theory and the practice of the subject are changing fast. The assumptions underlying the different theoretical frameworks are being revealed and questioned. New basic assumptions are being advocated, and consequently new frameworks constructed. One example is the theoretical framework of 'mental illness': the assumptions of normality and abnormality are being questioned, together with the notions of 'the cause', 'the cure', and 'the doctor–patient relationship'. As a result, different frameworks are developing, and different professional practices gradually being initiated. There are, though, various social and political structures which tend to inhibit the translation of changing theory into changing practice.

One interesting change is the current aversion to theoretical frameworks which liken human beings to something else. For example, among many psychologists the analogy of the human being as a computer which characterizes Unit A is in less favour than the concepts of development (Unit C) and the person (Unit D).

Essential Psychology as a whole is designed to reflect this changing structure and function of psychology. The authors are both academics and professionals, and their aim has been to introduce the most important concepts in their areas to beginning students. They have tried to do so clearly, but have not attempted to conceal the fact that concepts that now appear central to their work may soon be peripheral. In other words, they have presented psychology as a developing set of views of man, not as a body of received truth. Readers are not intended to study the whole series in order to 'master the basics'. Rather, since different people may wish to use different theoretical frameworks for their own purposes, the series has been designed so that each title stands on its own. But it is possible that if the reader has read no psychology before, he will enjoy individual books more if he has read the introductions (A1, B1 etc.) to the units to which they belong. Readers of the units concerned with applications of psychology (E, F) may benefit from reading all the introductions.

A word about references in the text to the work of other writers – e.g. 'Smith (1974)'. These occur where the author feels he must acknowledge an important concept or some crucial evidence by name. The book or article referred to will be listed in the bibliography (which doubles as name index) at the back of the book. The reader is invited to consult these sources if he wishes to explore topics further.

We hope you enjoy psychology.

Peter Herriot

And we are really here on a wonderful threshold of knowledge. The ascent of man is always teetering in the balance.
There is always a sense of uncertainty, whether when a man
lifts his foot for the next step it is really going to come down
pointing ahead. And what is ahead of us? At last the bringing
together of all that we have learned, in physics and biology,
towards an understanding of where we have come: what
man is.

J. Bronowski, *The Ascent of Man*, 1973: 436.

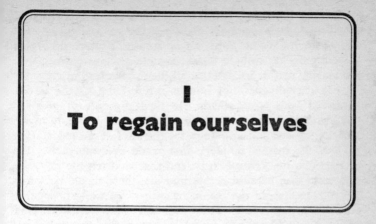

I
To regain ourselves

Surely it must be one of the most interesting things to be a psychologist at this particular juncture in human history. For now psychology seems to be involved in one of the most interesting and exciting developments in the whole nature of what it is to be a human being in the world – a development which it is the purpose of this book to discuss. There is a hope now that we can turn round our ability to grasp the reality of things to gain an understanding of our own *selves*; to understand (if not solve) the problem 'Why is I, I?'

Man, the self-defining animal

We begin our studies in psychology from the fact that our nature as human beings is a puzzle to us. But, we may ask, is that a puzzle we face just because we still remain ignorant about ourselves, because we have still not yet done enough research and amassed enough information about our behaviour? Or is it, perhaps, because we have no real nature, no natural nature, because we are self-determining, self-defining animals?

The latter notion is not such an outlandish one as it may at first sight seem; it is, after all, simply to restate the ideal embodied in the *humanism* of the Renaissance. We may turn to Pico della Mirandola's discourse *On the Dignity of Man* (1487, trans. Wallis, 1965) for an account of what constituted the humanistic attitude then. Mirandola begins his discourse by saying that he has studied all the various reasons given for the 'outstandingness' of human nature, and that he is dissatisfied with all of them. He then proceeds to give his definition of human nature by way of telling a story (a myth) about the creation. He suggests that, before he made man, 'God, the master builder', first made everything else, the world and the animals in it; and that God felt the necessity to make man because he 'desired that there should be someone to reckon up the reason of such a big work, to love its beauty, and to wonder at its greatness'. However, when God came to make man, he found that there was nothing in his 'archetypes' from which he could mould him; nor could God find a place in the world to put him. Thus:

> The best of workmen decided that that to which nothing of its very own could be given should be, in composite fashion given, whatsoever had belonged individually to each and everything. Therefore He took up man, a work of indeterminate form; and, placing him at the midpoint of the world, He spoke to him as follows: 'We have given thee, Adam, no fixed seat, no form of thy very own, no gift peculiarly thine, that thou mayest feel as thine own, have as thine own, possess as thine own the seat, the form, the gifts which thou thyself shalt desire.... Thou, like a judge appointed for being honourable, art the moulder and maker of thyself; thou mayest sculpt thyself into whatever shape thou dost prefer. Thou canst grow downwards into the lower natures which are brutes. Thou canst again grow upward from thy soul's reason into higher natures which are divine.'

For Mirandola, then, our puzzle about our nature was not just a matter of ignorance, a lack of knowledge: it was a real puzzle of a practical kind, for it was a puzzle about how we could transform ourselves from lower into higher forms.

And consider the transformations of man. The primeval state of man was hardly different as far as we can tell from that of today's apes. He lived then totally immersed in nature. Yet from being totally immersed in nature man is now all but surrounded by his own artefacts; from being hardly more skilful than the beasts he is now the possessor of countless bodily and mental skills. And this transformation has been brought about, it seems, solely by man himself. For 'there is no good evidence to support the assumption that man's neural system has undergone any progressive alteration in the direction of greater size or complexity since the middle of the Pleistocene (about 100,000 years ago)', says Mettler (1955, in Montague, 1962:197). Men have created and are still creating the characteristics of their own humanity. It has been produced, not as a result of evolutionary processes – processes that produce changes of a biological kind – for men seem to have stayed biologically constant for some time. Its development must be considered to be a historical, cultural one, a matter not of natural processes but of human imagination, choice and effort. And in 'inheriting' this manmade nature, this 'second nature', men's children do not inherit it genetically like blue eyes, but like the houses and the cities, the tools and the other more material artefacts of their parents and ancestors. They pass on to them the forms they have fashioned, and besides teaching them skill at using these they teach them skill at fashioning more. Children 'inherit' their humanity, then, in a process of communication which takes place after birth (Shotter, 1974a). There are no other species that have their forms of life communicated to them like this. It is this that makes man a being of rather a special kind.

What has been overlooked in modern psychology, especially in its more extreme mechanistic-behaviouristic manifestations as a natural science of behaviour, is that man is not simply a being immersed directly in nature but is a being *in a culture* in nature (see C3 of *Essential Psychology*). Thus people must not be treated like organisms that respond directly in relation to their position in the world, but as rather special organic forms which deal with nature in terms of their

13

knowledge of their 'position' in a culture; that is, in terms of a knowledge of the part their actions play in relation to the part played by other people's actions in maintaining (or progressing) the culture.

Now, objectively, of course, man is clearly just as much a part of nature as the trees and the stars. But equally clearly he thinks of himself as being in some way quite distinct from them. To an external observer many beings seem just as aware of their circumstances as man, just as *conscious* in that sense, we might say. So it must not just simply be by the mere possession, but by the *quality* of the consciousness that he possesses that man distinguishes himself from all else that there is. And to the extent that he can modify or transform the quality of his own consciousness he can modify or transform himself.

This, then, is the nature of the problem we currently face in psychology. Till now science has dealt only with objective forms and felt that it risked lapses into irrationality if it considered much else. Thus it studied only that which is 'outside' us, that which occurs independently of any responsibility that we could have for its behaviour. However, in psychology we *do* want to understand in what way we can be responsible for the behaviour of things, especially ourselves. Thus our problem is: can we construct a human science, just as rigorous and disciplined as a natural science, but which is concerned not with discovering the order and structure of things 'outside' us, but with the order and structure of things 'inside' us, in the intersubjectively shared meanings and understandings by which we live our lives? The answer I think is 'yes'. However, we must be prepared for some surprises: not only will its method and content be different from psychology as a natural science, its goal will be different too. Rather than prediction and control, it will seek *understandings*; so that by understanding more clearly what we are and the situation or 'position' we occupy, we may be able to describe explicitly the possibilities available to us all for what we might do next, for what we might make of ourselves and our world.

14

If men do make themselves, then, when they lose their grasp on quite how they do it, the process could miscarry, with both theoretical and practical consequences.

Theoretically, the aim of any science is to describe the unity and coherence of its subject matter. We cannot be content with merely accumulating in our journals an indefinitely long list of the empirical traits of man. Yet this is just what modern psychology does do. And in the attempt to find an 'organizing principle' it has taken up and then dropped one idea after another: reflexes, information theory, computer processes, etc., etc. – each new theoretical focus becoming a Procrustean bed into which the facts of man's supposed nature are meant to fit but will not.

The upshot of all this is that perhaps in no other age than ours has man become such a mystery to himself. We have a growing number of different social and biological sciences studying man, and psychology itself fragments almost daily into new specialist disciplines. Due to technological and conceptual advances, not only are we now able to do experiments and make observations that would have been inconceivable at the inception of scientific psychology, but our theories have also developed in surprising detail, scope and complexity. Compared with past ages, ours is indeed an affluent one. But to possess a wealth of facts is not necessarily to have a richness of understanding. The explosion in our knowledge has resulted in an ever expanding array of disconnected and fragmented data lacking all conceptual unity – it has provided material appropriate perhaps for the building of a great edifice, but no hint of a plan for its construction. Unless we can find a way of connecting all these scattered facts together, we shall remain buried under the debris of our own investigations. Thus we cannot begin in psychology as Newton began, 'by standing on the shoulders of giants'. Each new start we make begins (and ends) in the same way as the last – our psychology becomes like a merry-go-round, its tunes

15

and riders changing, but progress upon it largely an illusion.

But this fragmentation in our knowledge of ourselves is not merely a theoretical problem – it poses a threat to our whole ethical and cultural life. Without the proper processes by which culture is transmitted, without the respect for persons by which it is created and maintained, without a proper sense of the past and knowledge of real possibilities for the future, without an awareness of what is certain and what remains mysterious, the very effort to become human may miscarry. Has modern psychology done anything to combat this trend?

In a profoundly bitter, but surely now famous attack (one with which I would like to associate myself in its entirety), Koch (1964: 37–8) has described the unhappy influence of modern psychology as follows:

Modern psychology has provision for an ample margin of waste, especially of ideas. But nowhere can such 'give' in the system lead to less happy consequences than in psychology. For if psychology does not influence man's image of himself, what branch of scholarly community does? That modern psychology has projected an image of man which is as demeaning as it is simplistic, few intelligent and sensitive non-psychologists would deny. To such men – whether they be scientists, humanists or citizens – psychology has increasingly become an object of derision. *They* are safe even when most despairing. But for the rest, the mass dehumanization which characterizes our time – the simplification of sensibility, homogenization of experience, attenuation of the capacity for experience – continues apace. Of all fields in the community of scholarship, it should be psychology which combats this trend. Instead, we have played no small role in augmenting and supporting it. It should be a matter of embarrassment that the few who are effectively working against the deterioration of culture are the physicists, biologists, philosophers, historians, humanists, even administrators, participating in redefinition of knowledge to which I referred in my opening paragraphs

16

[referred to in this book on p. 69], but *not ourselves*. Is it not time that we raise the courage to relent?

But man's loss of grasp on himself is not something that has suddenly happened to him; his bewilderment at his own nature has been growing for some quite long time now. But recently, with the creation of modern psychology, it has reached the final stage in its growth, and the condition has now become acute. For we live in a scientific society, and yet our scientific scheme of things has no place in it for our selves; in scientific terms they have no reality at all.

The descent of man: from humanism to naturalism

Clearly, to man, the human world was (and for some still is) a special world, a unique world, a world in which men were there in the very centre of things, able themselves to act and to make things happen; it was *their* world. It is thus not surprising to find that it came as rather a shock to sixteenth-century sensibilities when Giordano Bruno, Copernicus and Galileo, one after another, insisted on removing man's world from the centre of things, and forced us all to accept that there were quite likely other worlds just like our own, and that we were more on the periphery of the cosmos than we had ever dreamed. Sensing the loss of something they felt precious to them, those in power at that time burnt Bruno, made Copernicus afraid to publish, and Galileo recant before the Inquisition. They feared that if one order of things could be so easily upset, then perhaps others could be also. And they were right. But the grasp on the reality of things provided by this new science was too much for them; but it was not gained without a certain cost in human suffering occasioned by people being unable to adapt themselves to the new schemes of things it produced.

Next to demote man from his special position in his world was Darwin. While Copernicus may have left men at the centre of things in *this* world, if not in the cosmos, Darwin

17

dissolved the line dividing men from animals. Thus men were reluctantly forced to accept that although they felt that they possessed divine souls, which was what made them distinct from the beasts, there was no scientific proof of their existence, whereas science did seem to show that men possessed many characteristics in common with animals. Again, men fought against accepting such a conclusion. But once again science triumphed by demonstrating that it had a greater grasp on the reality of things in the 'external world' than its opponents. In its behaviourist phase, appealing to Darwin and to the philosophy of science newly minted in the late nineteenth century, modern psychology completed man's assimilation into nature. After man's world had been reduced by Copernicus to a world like any other, man himself was reduced by Darwin to an organism like any other – except perhaps that he possessed speech (it remained to be seen whether that required special principles of explanation; in the event, it has proved to be the reductionist's stumbling block). In their turn, organisms were reduced to mechanisms like any others. And man became like everything else that there is in the world of the natural sciences: an assemblage of particles in motion according to laws – the particles, of course, all quite indistinguishable from one another. It is thus no wonder to find as a frontispiece in a recent (Open University) text in psychology, a design made up of a line of men, all faceless and identical to one another in every way, against a background of early computer machinery – the motif is stunningly accurate.

Men seek to know *themselves*, then, now perhaps more desperately than ever before. They want to be themselves among other selves, to know who and what they are in relation to others who are *like* themselves but not themselves. For even men born, say, as identical twins can and do become different selves. To be physically indistinguishable does not mean one cannot distinguish one's *self* from others. Thus men's selves are not to be identified with their physical bodies. Undoubtedly, it is a necessary condition of our being able to have selves that we do in fact have bodies, but we may con-

18

tinue to develop our selves long after what we think of as our bodies have ceased to grow.

Now men do not seek unique selves as a matter of vanity, in a merely frivolous attempt to be different. They want to know themselves in order to be able to ask – in order of increasing importance – questions such as the following: 'What are the things in *my* world?' 'What can *I* do to change things, to change my conditions?' 'What are the conditions in *my* world which make *me* like I am, and can I, in order to change myself, change them?' Unless we can formulate for ourselves an account of the world which has in it a proper place for our selves, it is of course difficult to give any rational answers to questions such as these.

'We' do not do all of what we are observed to do

Let me attempt to illustrate why the notion of *selves* is so important in human affairs by anticipating here some of the more detailed arguments to come in later chapters. Workers such as Fantz (1961) and Bower (1966; 1974), by using great experimental ingenuity, have demonstrated that very young children, sometimes only a few days old, show a great range of characteristic differential responses to their circumstances much earlier than we had ever expected before. They take their results, however, as indicating that babies 'know' in advance of experience how to do all kinds of things. But do they indicate this, do they indicate that the baby *himself* knows it?

Undoubtedly, if one is ingenious enough, one can use an infant as an extremely sensitive measuring instrument (or transducer) – much as canaries are used in mines to detect escapes of gas. As living organisms, existing in a state of exchange with their surroundings, presumably everything that happens near them causes some detectable change in babies' bodily states. But because an experimenter can detect a differential response in a child's behaviour, does that mean that the child himself can do so? To observe and characterize a baby's motions does not enable one to say that he *himself* has any *knowledge* of what he is doing. Something more is involved in people acting in the knowledge of who and what they are, and what they are trying to do in relation to the others with whom they share their lives, than merely behaving in a way *others* can recognize – one must be able, as Mead (1934) and Vygotsky (1966) point out, to recognize it *in the same way* oneself. The 'reflexive' quality of human action, its necessary reference to a *self*, is discussed extensively by Mead, as we shall see later.

It is thus one thing for an infant's activity to be thought of as a momentary result of a system of interdependent, interacting parts, and quite another for it to be considered as something for which he *himself* is responsible. While he might be considered by an outside observer to be an *organism*, acting as he must according to his bodily make up, he must also be considered as a *person*. For a forceful characterization of the distinction between the organic and the personal we may turn to Macmurray (1961: 49–50):

> In general, to represent the process of human development, even at its earliest stage, as an organic process, is to represent it in terms which are equally applicable to the development of animals, and therefore to exclude reference to rationality in any of its expressions, practical or theoretical; reference to action or to knowledge, to deliberate purpose or reflective thought. If this were correct, no infant could ever survive. For its existence and its development depend from the beginning on rational activities, upon thought and action. The baby cannot yet think or act. Consequently, he must depend for his life upon the thought and action of others. The conclusion is not that the infant is still an animal which will become rational through some organic process of development. It is that he cannot, even theoretically, live an isolated existence; that he is not an independent individual. He lives a common life as one term in a personal relation.

For evidently on some occasions at least he can act, not as

his immediate bodily states demand, but on the contrary in relation to needs and interests which must be characterized *in other people's terms*, not just his own. To become a socially responsible agent, the child must learn, then, not just to control his own behaviour and to control it intelligently in relation to his own needs, but to control it intelligibly and responsibly. He must learn to control it in a way that makes sense to others and relates in some way with what, overall, others are trying to do in their lives.

Thus these brilliant researches may certainly be revealing what is 'there' in the child for him himself to call on, but the task of understanding how he learns to use what is 'there' in a way that makes sense to others still remains. We ourselves, then, do not necessarily do all we are observed to do; we must distinguish between that which we intend and that which merely happens. Even as adults we may still find ourselves (or be found by others) to be reacting to situations in all kinds of as yet unrecognized and indescribable ways, and these reactions are 'there' in us as vague intuitions of something possibly new about the situations to be discovered. And there is a process of discovery which elucidates such intuitions; it consists in working out ways of giving them clear and adequate expression – as, for instance, Chomsky (1965) has done, at least to a degree, for what were otherwise our vague intuitions about the structure of grammatical sentences. Such a transition, from vague origins to more detailed and refined consequences, is involved in the dialectical developmental process that I shall describe later – a process in which spontaneous activity is transformed into deliberate activity (into actions a person himself can *decide* to do) in the course of instruction *by another person* (Vygotsky, 1962; 1966).

To make more of our 'selves'

This book, then, is offered as a contribution to a very general attempt which I feel is being made in many other quarters at the present time: the attempt to regain what many feel we

21

have nearly lost – our selves. To some, those like Skinner (1972) or Eysenck (1969), who feel that our hope for the future lies in the discovery of technologies for the manufacture of deliberately designed cultures to replace our current, confused ways of going on, the appeals here will seem old-fashioned – even perhaps, as Broadbent (1973) has termed them, 'the last kicks of an outdated culture'. For such people believe that it is not man's idolatry of the natural sciences that has anything to do with our current problems. It is, they feel, our belief in human dignity, and the literature of freedom, that has encouraged us not to submit our selves to the appropriate controls, and has thus brought us to our current pass.

I hope to show, however, that the appeals here are not in any sense old-fashioned ones at all; that in fact we are now on the brink of a great new development quite inconceivable within our past ideas of scientific achievement: the possibility that we can begin now to investigate how men enter into the processes of their own development, and thus to discover what we might make of ourselves more than we already are.

What this book is about

This book, then, is on images of man in psychological research, and in it I want to do two things. First, in a rather discursive account of what I take to be the standard classical approach in psychology at the moment (the study of man as a mechanism from a standpoint as an external observer), I shall attempt to distinguish three *forms of order*, each consisting of a system of interrelated descriptive categories: the mechanical, the organic, and the personal. Second, I shall also discuss in the course of the account the different *standpoints* we might take while studying man in relation to these three forms of order.

The discussion of standpoints is perhaps even more crucial than that of the forms of order, as it has to do with the criteria we use in assessing the accuracy of our theoretical accounts. As I have already indicated, we may take a standpoint as an individual, as an external observer, using only observational and formal (see discussion of Galileo in Chapter 3) criteria in testing our theories. We might instead, but it is not yet a part of science to do so, take a standpoint not as external observers but as agents immersed in the action we are studying, referring not to observational but to experiential criteria in testing our theories. We might go even further and take a standpoint, not just as individual agents, but as socially responsible agents, judging by criteria shared by all others in our community. This would shift the classical starting point for any sort of theoretical account of things, first from thought to action, and then from an egocentric to a social standpoint – a shift in standpoint, from one in scholarly reflection to one in everyday social practices. That is the standpoint I shall argue for in this book (Macmurray, 1957; 1961).

What follows, then, is an essay in theoretical psychology, concerned first with justifying the need for a new approach (a new form of order plus a new standpoint), and then with an attempt to provide it. It emphasizes the importance of the cultural, the historical and the social aspects of man rather than the more classical scientific concerns with the natural, the organic and the biological. It thus proposes a psychology which is a *moral science of action* rather than a *natural science of behaviour*. The essay, however, at very best must be considered as merely an introduction to such a new form of psychology. For between establishing the vague outlines of a new approach and the construction in detail of a refined, systematic, disciplined study, lies the task of gradually working through and checking out in concrete detail all the implications of the new concepts – that is, if its value is to be rationally appraised at all. That task here is hardly begun.

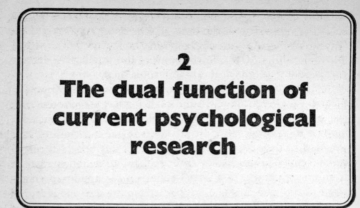

2
The dual function of current psychological research

Psychological research can be influential in human affairs, it is thought, if it can discover, scientifically, facts about human behaviour, and from such facts develop behavioural technologies, ways of achieving the goals we desire. In this chapter I want to examine another way in which psychological research may be influential: its effect on our image of ourselves. And I want to do this for two reasons: first to explore the hidden influences of current research in psychology, and second to suggest that this type of influence is its most important consequence. For if psychological research can indeed have a great influence in human affairs, it is clearly desirable to understand how these effects are achieved, if for no other reason than for us to be able to use its power wisely rather than have it produce all kinds of disturbances in our lives accidentally.

Psychology's influence on our image of ourselves

In 1969, in response to the social and political pressures which were then acute in America but still now continue, the American Psychological Association took as its annual conference theme 'Psychology and the problems of society'. In accord with the conference theme, George A. Miller, who was the Association's president at the time, took as the title of his address 'Psychology as a means of promoting human welfare' (Miller, 1969). I will let Miller do the work of introducing the hidden function of psychological research to us now.

On the one hand, few now doubt the importance of psychological research in human affairs – if for no other reason than that society has few other directions in which to turn for guidance and direction than to the social sciences in general and psychology in particular. On the other hand, it is difficult to pinpoint the way in which it can have its effect. Certainly, as a behavioural science, Miller feels that psychology is one of the most revolutionary enterprises ever conceived by the mind of man. 'If we were ever to achieve substantial process toward our stated aim', he says, 'toward the understanding, prediction, and control of mental and behavioural phenomena – the implications for every aspect of society would make brave men tremble' (1969:1065). It would, that is, were there any signs of this revolution coming to pass. But there are not. One is forced to admit that scientific psychology has not achieved anything that seems to be at all revolutionary, Miller feels. Yet he goes on to say, 'I do not believe the psychological revolution is pie in the sky. It has already begun' (1969:1066). It exists and is with us now. The reason it has not been more obvious is that we have been looking for it in the wrong place.

Traditionally, one expects scientific investigations to result, at a practical level, in new technologies, in new ways of manipulating our circumstances to make them accord more with our desires. Scientists are thus thought of as discovering the means to ends which others – the public, the representatives of the public, or, perhaps, other wealthy and powerful interests – may decide to use or not as the case may be. But, says Miller, 'I believe that the real impact of psychology will be felt, not through the technological products it places in the hands of powerful men, but through its effects on the public at large, through a new and different public conception of what is humanly possible and what is humanly desirable' (1969: 1066).

25

Rather than discovering means to ends, it may work to influence the whole character of the ends with which we concern ourselves in our lives. Thus modern psychology, although it may present itself as working on just one front – as an experimental science of behaviour – it actually seems to work on two fronts at once: explicitly but rather unsuccessfully as a natural science, implicitly and rather more successfully to change our images of ourselves. Let me discuss these two spheres of activity in turn.

Image realization and image replacement

Explicitly, we can think of modern psychology as working on what I would like to call image realization; that is, given a particular image of man's nature, it works to discover, or to realize in behaviour, the possibilities inherent in it. For instance, assuming that in at least some situations men may operate as 'limited capacity information channels', it may set out to explore, behaviourally, the implications of such an assumption as this (Broadbent, 1958). None of the investigations would function to prove that man is nothing but an 'information channel', they would just show what is possible when men act as if they were one. This is the best, it seems to me, for reasons which will become apparent as this book progresses, that psychology in its guise as a behavioural science can do; it cannot, as it hopes, penetrate into men's actual inner 'workings', for it can never escape from the fact that we only ever investigate what we mean by the term 'our inner workings'. And while the meaning of the term may be changed as a result of our investigations, even then we still confront what we mean by the term rather than our actual inner workings 'in themselves'.

But if one disagrees with this and feels that such experimental work can reveal something very fundamental about the nature of man, one ought to remember that men in such experiments usually consent to act as the experimenter asks. They do so, presumably, because they believe in the value of helping scientists to make discoveries. It is thus rather un-appreciative of experimenters to tell their subjects, once an experiment is over, that because they acted as a theory had predicted, they are in fact nothing but mechanisms working with logical principles. That is not the case at all. In choosing to help the experimenter, a subject agrees to view the situation in which he is placed as the experimenter asks. And it would not be surprising to find that, unless the experimenter has purposely misled him, he views it in the same rational light as the experimenter himself, considering just the very aspects of it the experimenter himself considered in formulating his theory. It is thus not at all surprising to find him acting as the theory predicts. And it is not because he has no choice in the matter. On the contrary. It is just because he does have a choice in the matter that he acts as he does.

Explicitly, then, as a behavioural science, psychology may work to reveal what follows at a practical level when men choose to go on in one way rather than another. But besides work of this kind, modern psychology may be thought of as having something to do with what I want to call image re-placement. That is, instead of working to clarify and help in the practical realization of our already 'given' but admittedly rather vague image of ourselves as *persons*, it works to bring in new notions to replace such everyday ideas. But it does this implicitly rather than explicitly, for it does it only incidentally in the course of conducting itself as a science, not as a part of its professed aim at all. In fact, to put up an image of ourselves for discussion before the conduct of experimental analysis is to be accused of doing 'armchair psychology', of engaging in metaphysical speculation uselessly. In 1879, in establishing itself as an experimental science, psychology de-termined to sever itself from philosophy and to concern itself, primarily, with the experimentally established facts of human nature. So while theories may be used in an attempt to explain the facts once they have been established, scientifically, it is not acceptable to theorize before the facts are in.

Yet this is just what psychology does do (and cannot avoid doing). And the trouble is that in presenting its results as scientifically valid ones – results obtained, say, on the hypothesis that man operates like an 'information channel' (see A5) – implicit acceptance is gained for the underlying hypothesis. Such results come to be taken, not as indicating what men might be like (how they might make themselves act), but as indicating what in fact they are like. The image of man implicit in the results is transmitted and established along with the results. And psychologists come to argue, not just that we should think about ourselves and others in new ways, but that we should treat one another in new ways because they are ways with a scientifically established reality to them – something our notion of ourselves as persons lacks. And this may happen as a result of work in different spheres of psychology irrespective of whether the results in those spheres are of scientifically satisfactory character or not. It can happen just as a result of suggesting that men should be thought of as being entities of one kind rather than another in order to investigate them in a scientific manner. 'We are what we pretend to be', says Kurt Vonnegut Jun. (1968), 'So we must be careful about what we pretend to be.'

Understanding problems rather than providing solutions

Miller (1969) notes in this connection the effects of Freud's theories on Western society. He believes that it is impossible to argue that their effects have been achieved because they provided new means for achieving desired goals. 'As a method of therapy', says Miller, 'Psychoanalysis has had limited success even for those who can afford it. It has been more successful as a method of investigation, perhaps, but even there it has only been one of several available methods. The impact of Freud's thought has been due far less to the instrumentalities he provided than the changed conception of ourselves that he implied' (1969:1067). Freud did not provide us with any clear solutions to the problems we face; one might even say that he added to them. But as a result of changing the way in which we think about ourselves, we now face quite different problems from those faced by men before Freud. It is in this way that psychology might exert its most powerful influence, especially if, as Miller notes right at the beginning of his address, 'the most urgent problems of our world are the problems we have made for ourselves' (1969 : 1063).

Man over against or in the world

I would like to endorse Miller's view of psychology's dual function, and I shall try to explore in this book most of the images of man implicit in the recent and current psychological research, and the reasons they took the form that they did. As a foretaste of this, however, let me outline two great images of man which differ in almost every detail. One is the image that seems to me to have informed and structured most of the work in psychology for at least the last hundred years, the other has yet to gain serious attention.

The classical image of man presented to modern psychology by modern philosophy, but obviously inherited by us from the Greeks, is of man as a thinking subject set over against the world as an object. Currently, man must view himself either as a non-material mind quite separated from a material world (which contains among other things, his own body), or as a special form of causal nexus all in the material world, held together by his bodily envelope, i.e. as simply a material object of great complexity. Rather than the former dualist view, modern psychology has opted, at least so it claims, for the latter, materialist view. Either way, 'we' are left puzzled as to our place in the real world, for man has no obvious place in the material world for his apparently non-material but nonetheless very real self. Furthermore, in such circumstances, it is difficult to understand the task we face in such a world. As a material body, we presumably have no task, for our feeling that there are things we ought to be trying to do in order to promote human welfare can only be an illusion, for the activities of bodies are caused by events external to them. And as a mind, quite separate from the world as matter, the task of man as a thinker can only be that of discovering a 'view' of how the world really is, thus hoping in some unexplained way to gain a sort of technical mastery over it (unexplained, since the relation between thought and action, like that between body and mind, is left a mystery). This, at least, was the great hope expressed by Descartes. He suggested that

> ... by knowing the force and action of fire, water, air, the stars, the heavens, and all other bodies that surround us ... we should be able to utilize them for all the uses to which they are suited and thus render ourselves masters and possessors of nature.

And this is just what we have been attempting to do for the last 350 years; we have been attempting to render ourselves masters and possessors of nature by conceiving of it as consisting of elementary and independent particles of matter in blind but lawful motion, and by searching for these elements and the principles governing their motions. And as this 'scientific' mode of thought has grown to be the ideal for all valid modes of thought, we have tried to bring into its confines what Descartes had quite explicitly left out: our 'rational souls' – in other words, ourselves as rational agents. Like all other activity in the material world, we are now trying to explain men's actions in terms of viewing him as a submechanism within the great mechanism of nature.

The classical view of man, then, is at once a view of him as an isolated, thinking subject set over against an objective world, facing an essentially theoretical task, and a view of him as a mechanism, operating according to laws. Epistemologically, we feel that the only form of real knowledge we can have about the world is that which we have in thought, reflection or contemplation, i.e. objective knowledge. And, ontologically, everything that exists in the world as we know it exists as an entity constituted from a determinate set of independent elements in lawful motion.

As an alternative to this classical view of man as primarily an isolated and egocentric contemplative, separated from the world of practical affairs, we may view him as primarily a doer, immersed in the world as an *agent*, who has the power to act on the world and to change it to accord more with his own needs and interests. Rather than a being able to exist in isolation from all else that there is, we may view him as an organism, relying for his existence on living in a state of exchange with his surroundings – being able to influence them but also being influenced by them. But even more than this: we may consider him as living in the world in a state of exchange with other agents both like and unlike himself, forming *communities* such that together they can do more than they could ever do alone. As an agent immersed in the world with other agents in community with them, man faces the task, as we have said before, of acting not just intelligently, but intelligibly and responsibly. Thus, even if he is quite alone when acting, he must be able to evaluate his own actions as he performs them, in other people's terms – this, as we shall see, is part of what it is to be able to say that he himself is responsible for his own actions. This then is the task of man as a socially responsible agent immersed in a community in the world with other agents like himself: unlike the task of man the thinker, his task is to give intelligible form to the world, his life, and the living of it, not simply to describe it; it is a practical not a theoretical task. Such an image of man involves not only a shift in standpoint from one in thought to another in action, it is also an intrinsically social view of man. Rather than an egocentric self, it is a view of man as a person among other persons, a self with a persona, a way of presenting himself to other selves.

Giving psychology away to those who need it

Having now introduced in outline an alternative to the classical view of man, I would like now to mention one more point made by Miller (1969) in comparing the two functions of research in modern psychology: as a natural science, psychology aims theoretically at providing the true view of man's psychological nature, and practically at applying the theoretical principles discovered to provide behavioural technologies. These are aims that psychologists as experts, as professionals, can attain on their own, presenting their results to the public at large as and when they obtain them. This was indeed the hope that Watson (1913) expressed for behaviourism: 'If psychology would follow the plan I suggest', he said in his very original paper on behaviourism, 'The educator, the physician, the jurist and the businessman could utilize our data in a practical way, as soon as we are able, experimentally, to obtain them.' Miller, however, as we shall see, is unhappy with the idea of psychologists as experts.

The alternative view of man that I have been discussing above will, I shall show, like the classical view, support a science. But it will be a science of quite a different kind from that of physics and the other natural sciences with which we are familiar. It will lead to what I shall call a moral science: it will be concerned with, as Miller says, 'conceptions of what is humanly possible and what is humanly desirable'. In other words, it will be concerned not with seeing deeply into the inner workings of things and discovering their rock bottom, ultimate causes, but with our options as to how to live. And I feel justified in claiming that such an enterprise can be called a scientific one as I take it that what distinguishes those activities we designate as 'scientific' and mark off from the rest of what we do is that in them we attempt to discover general principles by which we can transform ourselves from being victims to being masters of our fates. Some may object to this, and say that psychology is a science because it uses scientific methods, and I have not proposed, and neither shall I propose, any methods like the methods in the natural sciences (I shall, however, propose some methods). But an activity does not necessarily become a science just because it uses scientific methods in its conduct. Scientific methods may be used for all sorts of purposes other than scientific ones – that is their value and their danger. Doing science is doing your utmost with whatever one has got to improve one's grasp on the reality of things; it is difficult to argue that there is any one single method of doing that. Empirically, all that matters is that the verifiable consequences of our proposed accounts are such that experience will confirm them.

Taking this more personal attitude to science, though, changes more than just the theoretical conception of its aim – it changes its practice also. It can no longer be conducted just by experts, and the results, once obtained, then handed on to the educators, jurists, etc., for there are no such results of that kind! The results it produces cannot be used as recipes for action for they are merely shared, or *intersubjective understandings*. Now it is understanding that Miller feels should be psychology's goal: without giving any sort of account of an alternative psychology which might be productive of understanding rather than control, he nevertheless argues that 'understanding and prediction are better goals for psychology and for the promotion of human welfare – because they lead us to think, not in terms of coercion by a powerful elite, but in terms of the diagnosis of problems and the development of programs that can enrich the lives of every citizen' (1969: 1069).

But there is a problem, a problem Miller discusses at some length: if psychologists are not going to be experts applying psychology to the rest of us, how can psychology be 'given away' to those who need it? This is a problem of practice, not of theory, of how psychological research can be conducted. 'People are growing increasingly alienated', says Miller, 'from a society in which few wise men behind closed doors decide what is good for everyone' (1969: 1074). Thus, although I want to argue in this book that we are now on the threshold of understanding man himself in a way never before possible in the past, it is still not enough. It is one thing to grasp an exciting new theory; it is quite another to realize it in practice in everyday life. Powerful elites may attempt to realize their theories using different forms of coercion, subtle or otherwise; psychologists as psychologists should not, I feel, participate in such attempts. It should not be just the psychologist's job to realize his theories in practice. We all must take his theories and use them as and when we can, as we each individually and corporately find them appropriate. The invention of a social structure in which the divisions between psychologists and non-psychologists are broken down, and the task of helping people at large to be their own psychologists (see F4) is an adventure to which we all as psychologists may look forward. 'So let us', says Miller, at the end of his address, 'continue our struggle to advance psychology as a means of promoting human welfare, each in our own way. For myself, however, I can imagine nothing more relevant to human welfare, and nothing that could pose a greater challenge to the next generation of psychologists, than to discover how best to give psychology away' (1969: 1074).

For my own part, I can only say that at the moment I do not know how this goal is going to be achieved. The best that I feel I can do at the moment is to try to construct a theory and a method (and a good reason) for understanding men, in an attempt to make such an enterprise as giving psychology away both an intelligible and worthwhile one.

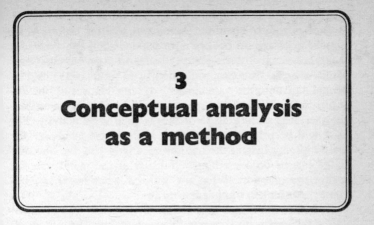

3
Conceptual analysis
as a method

Attempting to achieve Miller's goal of 'giving away' psychology, I shall take it that instead of trying to replace our ordinary, everyday concepts and concerns with others – ones more amenable to experimental analysis, perhaps, but otherwise rather unfamiliar to ordinary people – psychologists ought to leave them as they are and make an attempt to understand them. Thus psychology must begin, not by doing experiments to establish 'the facts', but by clarifying our ordinary everyday concepts of ourselves and others as persons; especially, as we shall discover in this chapter, that 'facts' are determined as what they are by the conceptual frameworks within which they are gathered.

Conceptual problems

As this book does not seek a link between theory and practice via experimentation (see A1), but attempts to establish a much more direct link between conceptual matters and the structure of everyday life, it will be rather different to most of the other books in the other sections of this series, and it will thus require a rather different attitude of mind in reading it. In other psychology texts, conceptual issues, if they are mentioned at all, are discussed in relation to theories under experimental test. Thus, for instance, conflicting experimental results may force psychologists to ask one another about what they really mean by the terms, say, 'short-term memory' and 'iconic storage' (see A6), and whether, in terms of the experimental situation, they are close or distant relatives of one another. So, although experimentalists do indulge in conceptual analyses, it is something secondary to their main activity. For us it will be primary. This is because we are taking as our main task, not that of the natural scientist asking the question 'How can we do something?' but that of the moral scientist asking the question 'What are we and what might we become?' A problem of ends not means.

Now it is important to understand what this task of elucidating the important concepts by which we regulate our everyday life entails, because it is a task quite different from that of the experimentalists. What if we were to ask, following Winch (1958), whether the mind of man can have any contact with 'reality' at all, and if it can, what difference can we expect it to make in his life? Such a question cannot be settled by experimental methods, for it is not an empirical question in any sense. It is a conceptual one. 'It has to do', says Winch, 'with the force of the concept of reality. An appeal to the results of an experiment would necessarily beg the important question, since the philosopher would be bound to ask by what token those results themselves are accepted as "reality"' (1958:9). The task is not one of proving whether reality exists or not, but of making clear what one commits oneself to saying or doing in the future by saying now that it exists. To clarify one's concept of reality, one has to show what follows in practice, if one were to act upon it – meanings of terms are elucidated by making the practical implications of using such terms clear. So, for instance, here in this book, among other things, we shall be asking what in practice does it mean to say that people are best treated as people, or as organisms, or as machines; it is in terms of what it implies for future action that the meaning of a term is specified. Thus, if I am to establish that my concept of reality is in fact the

36

same as yours, we must both check (either in imagination or actuality) the ways that we apply our concepts in a wide range of practical situations, making sure that we do indeed both apply our concepts in the same way. If we do not agree on what counts for us as something being real, then it will be clear that we disagree as to what we think 'reality' is, and to what one should refer when one uses the term.

Conceptual analysis is thus an important endeavour, for it has to do with clarifying what counts for us as our world at this particular moment in history. Without such an agreed framework of meanings and implications within which the currently known facts about ourselves and our world can be placed in a proper relation to one another – a framework of intersubjectively shared understandings – it is not at all clear what is required of further investigations, what should be sought and by what means. As a preliminary to any scientific inquiry, we must try to state clearly and agree upon what it is that we are investigating, such that we all may coordinate our inquiries into it in a disciplined manner.

Given the centrality of our language in all of this, it is important to be clear about the relation between our world, especially our social world, and our language. Now there are some theories of language which suggest that language and all the rest of what there is in the world, including our thoughts, are quite distinct and separate from one another; that, on the one hand, there are things – objects, human relationships, concepts, thoughts, etc. – which we know about in some sort of direct way, and, on the other hand, there is a codified form of expression which can be learnt and used independently of dealing with the world, practically and socially. This is the theory that words simply 'stand for' things, or that language 'mirrors' the world (see A7). But as a matter of fact, one does not learn one's language independently of dealing with the world in a social context. 'What is missed', says Winch (1958: 44) in discussing the simple theory of language above, 'is that ... categories of meaning, etc., are logically dependent for their sense on social interaction between men.' The meanings we express in our language and the way in which we act in our everyday practices are woven into one another. Literally, meanings are a part of our ways of going on, for they 'point to', given what we are doing now, what we could go on to try to do in the future – if we see our actions as having any meaning, that is. Thus it is that Winch comments:

> We cannot say ... that the problems of philosophy arise out of language *rather than* out of the world, because in discussing language philosophically we are in fact discussing *what counts as belonging to the world*. Our idea of what belongs to the world is given to us in the language that we use. The concepts we have settle for us the form of the experience we have in the world. It may be worth reminding ourselves of the truism that when we speak of the world we are speaking of what we in fact mean by the expression 'the world': there is no way of getting outside the concepts in terms of which we think of the world ... The world is for us what is presented through these concepts. That is not to say, our concepts may not change; but when they do, that means that our concept of the world has changed too. (1958:15)

And many issues in the social sciences, Winch argues, belong more to philosophy than to science and are, therefore, to be settled by *a priori* conceptual analysis rather than by further empirical research; they are matters of ordering and clarifying what we already know, rather than matters of factual ignorance. For, after all, they bear not on matters of natural necessity, but upon what the way of going on we determined for ourselves in the past means for us now. Thus, for example, 'the question of what constitutes social behaviour', says Winch (1958:18), 'is a demand for an elucidation of the *concept* of social behaviour. In dealing with questions of this sort there should be no question of "waiting to see" what empirical research will show us; it is a matter of tracing the implications of the concepts we use.' What we think of ourselves as trying to do in carrying on our relationships with other people is an important determinant in influencing what we actually do, whether we succeed in our aims or not.

Finally, let me comment here upon the definition of concepts. It is all too easy, in talking about concepts as things, to feel that we are talking about objects that can be defined by describing their structure. But we must remember that while concepts may seem to be objective things, we make and continually remake them within ourselves. We shall mislead ourselves if, for instance, we think of any of our concepts (except those artificially closed to further innovative development in systems of logic, in calculi, and in games like chess) as having well-defined structure to them. 'We are unable clearly to circumscribe the concepts we use', says Wittgenstein (1958:25), 'not because we don't know their real definition, but because there is no real "definition" to them. To suppose that there must be would be like supposing that whenever children play with a ball they play a game according to strict rules.' The best we can do is to clarify what our concepts seem to be now. As a result of further investigations and other human affairs, events and happenings, they may be very different in the future.

Intersubjectively shared meanings and understandings

Before effective scientific research can begin, as Kuhn (1962, p. 4) points out, a scientific community must settle amongst itself answers to questions like the following: (1) What are the fundamental entities which constitute its subject matter? (2) How do these interact with one another, and with the human senses? (3) What questions may be legitimately asked about such entities, and what techniques employed in seeking solutions to them? And finally to Kuhn's list, as in this case our subject matter is ourselves, as persons, we must add: (4) understanding how many findings that we might make reflect back upon and modify our original concept of ourselves as persons.

Now psychology does not have yet, I think, general answers to these questions, and is thus not yet in a position to do effective scientific research. And there are two things that it is no use psychologists complaining about when psychology is criticized in this sort of way. First, it is no use them protesting – on almost every other page of their books – that they are in fact doing science because they are using scientific methods. As I have already pointed out, to use scientific methods is not necessarily to do science; to use the tools of a trade is not necessarily to practice that trade. And, secondly, it is no use experimental psychologists complaining that the philosophical activity needed to clarify its concepts is speculative philosophy 'through the armchair'. For, as they should know only too well, making observations and doing experiments has nothing to do with discovering statements : experiments are only meant to put the logically derived consequences of clear statements to the test. The formulation by a scientific community of concepts and theories for use in the regulation of their empirical investigations is a matter for discussion amongst themselves about their concepts, not about their empirical findings. Such findings are supposed to settle matters beyond dispute. In 1879, by putting a taboo upon anything other than experimentation, psychology lost its independence from philosophical speculation at the very moment it declared it – for it then lumbered itself with a speculative philosophy which, although long since outmoded, has remained unchanged through remaining unexamined.

Our concern with clarifying concepts, then, has to do with clarifying the frameworks of thought within which scientific statements may be formulated and from which they draw their significance, and there is no straightforward way in which empirical facts could be said either to verify or falsify such frameworks. For they lay down the ground rules that scientists use in identifying what needs explaining and what counts as an intelligible explanation. So, what we elucidate in conceptual analysis are the shared frameworks of meaning within which we interpret the significance of what we do and what we experience.

Now, later I shall argue that man is not to be known for what he is in terms of any objective criteria, for objectively he is as much a part of nature as anything else. It is by the character of his consciousness that he distinguishes himself from all else that there is; he thinks of himself as distinct, and in so thinking acts as if he is a distinct form of being. So any science concerned with man as an entity distinct from the rest of what there is in nature, with man as a being not directly in nature but relating himself to it via a culture, must possess a way of characterizing the qualities of man's consciousness. It is by the intersubjective meanings or understandings implicit in people's practices that the quality of people's consciousness in a culture may be characterized. The idea of *intersubjectivity*, the notion of a shared system of concepts and their implications giving a meaning to all that happens in a society, thus becomes a central term in any science of consciousness (Taylor, 1971; O'Neill, 1974). And of central importance in such a system is our intersubjectively shared concept of ourselves.

Image explication

What we are attempting to do in conceptual analysis, then, is this: rather than trying to find out, experimentally, more and fresh empirical traits of human nature, we are trying to bring to the surface and remove the contradictions existing in what we already know about ourselves as persons. And surely, we already know a great deal, in practice if not in theory: we do not, for instance, continually mistake other things for people, we do not expect them to have all the sorts of abilities possessed by people; while, on the other hand, we do expect people to respond to us, to try to communicate, to perceive, to remember, understand and so on. In practice at least, we act towards machines, organisms and people in quite distinct ways, and, for all practical intents and purposes, face few problems in discriminating which is which. In our everyday relationships we do not continually confuse and baffle one another; it is only in theory that we find we cannot say, clearly, what the difference is. Thus, we cannot formulate statements of how we do in fact distinguish ourselves from all else that there is by doing experiments; instead we have to catch ourselves in the act, so to speak, and try to make clear to ourselves the ways in which, in practice, we make the distinctions we do. There clearly must be some basis somewhere for the orderly ways in which we can act. It is our task in conceptual analysis to bring that basis out into the light of day.

The process involved in conceptual analysis is, then, neither image realization nor image replacement but image explication. Both the former rely heavily upon imaginative theoretical constructions, asking the question 'What might man be like?' Image explication is the attempt to characterize as clearly and as systematically as possible the character of an intuition, the sense which we have of ourselves as we act and which seems in some way to guide what we try to do. In so doing, it draws on our experiences of ourselves rather than upon any observations that we might make, as outsiders, of others.

The undisciplined theorizing of the behavioural sciences

Currently, theorizing in the behavioural sciences proceeds in an utterly undisciplined manner. While attempts have been made time and again to frame criteria for the formulation of scientifically adequate hypotheses, no criteria exist at all for the formulation of hypotheses adequate to man, our subject matter. If any rule exists at all, it is that concepts drawn from everyday modes of speech are deemed quite inappropriate to any exact grasp of the human situation. It is maintained that those who attempt to use everyday language in psychological contexts introduce unnecessary confusions and that a technical vocabulary, based on the results of an experimental analysis of 'the way people work' (Broadbent, 1969: 40), is more appropriate. Thus experimental psychologists draw concepts 'ready made' from almost any handy source but our intuitions of ourselves.

The reason for their fear of our intuitions can be found in the biases introduced into psychology by its attempt to make itself into a natural science like physics, so it is to a prelim-

42

inary examination of these biases that we now turn (they are further examined in Chapter 5).

Just as in primitive atomic theory it was thought that all atoms had to be indistinguishable and colourless (the different properties of things being explained in terms of the different possible arrangements of atoms), so in psychology it was thought necessary to begin with psychologically neutral components, the different behavioural functions resulting from their special arrangements. Thus, says Hull:

> An ideally adequate theory even of so called purposive behaviour ... ought to begin with colourless movement and mere receptor impulses as such, and from these build up step by step both adaptive and maladaptive behaviour. (1943:25)

And so, instead of starting with fundamental psychological facts and attempting to elucidate the relations between them, thus forming them into a system with all its attendant explanatory advantages, these facts themselves constituted what was to be explained. Hull did not deny consciousness, but instead of furnishing a means for the solution of psychological problems he felt that its existence was itself a problem needing solution. Others had tried to array some fundamental psychological facts upon which to found a psychology (as I shall again try in Chapter 6):

> The most general and fundamental facts about experience ... are two. First, experience or experiencing is always an experience of *something* ... Secondly, all experiencing ... is the experiencing of *someone*, some subject, some person, some organism. (McDougall, 1923:40)

However, the insistence of the behaviourists prevailed; for only their proposals seemed to satisfy the requirements of science. But, one feels forced to ask, 'Were their theories ideally adequate because science is science or because man is man?'

The question is all the more relevant because we have still not yet solved the problem of what our fundamental units

43

ought to be. Obliged by its adoption of the methods of the natural sciences to search for some fundamental elements from which to build the mechanisms to mediate between our circumstances and our behaviour, psychology has taken up and then dropped model after model. Models from science laboratories, workshops, computer rooms, and many other sources have been taken up as representatives of man's processes and their properties explored. Enthusiasm has waned as their partial character has become apparent. As there have been no criteria for judging the worth of such proposals, the content of such theorizing has been quite undisciplined. A psychology based in an experimental analysis of 'the way people work', although perhaps instrumentally effective, is no more a completely rational endeavour than the speculative philosophy it claimed to replace.

The next two chapters will give added support to that statement. In Chapter 4 we shall examine the attempt to find psychology's 'atoms', and how the need to give an account of the 'whole' man seems to defeat every effort. And in Chapter 5 we shall turn to an examination of the very fundamental biases and presuppositions in the classical scientific approach to show that powerful though the natural sciences may be, their origins are speculative; we are not of necessity bound to accept the framework of thought they provide. We may then, as psychologists, feel free to invent another, one more adequate for our own subject matter: man (Shotter, 1974b).

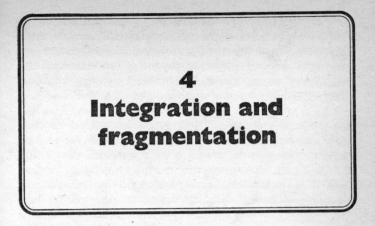

4
Integration and fragmentation

Later, in Chapter 6, I shall assert, and give some reasons why psychology should be the disciplined study of our intuitive sense of ourselves as persons, which is one thing that distinguishes it from all the other scientific disciplines that there are: it has a subject matter unlike any other. However, as a behavioural science, psychology has not found it easy to distinguish itself from other sciences: many of them could be said to be concerned with man's functioning in one way or another. Joynson (1970; 1972; Harré, 1971) has discussed this matter, and it is from his papers that I draw the first part of my discussion here.

Joynson's dilemma

As a discipline concerned with the study of man and his nature, the stock answer to the question of how it is distinguished from other closely related disciplines is now and has always been that psychology concerns itself with the *whole* man, the integrated individual. Thus Watson (1924) writes:

Behaviourism ... is, then, a natural science that takes the whole field of human adjustment as its own. Its closest scientific companion is physiology. Indeed you may wonder, as we proceed, whether behaviourism can be differentiated from that science. It is different from physiology only in the grouping of its problems ... physiology is particularly interested in the functioning of parts of the animal.... Behavourism ... is intrinsically interested in what the whole animal will do from morning till night.... (1924:24)

And others too, Joynson points out, attempt to distinguish psychology in this way. But is this good enough, for physiologists are also often interested in the coordinated functioning of parts of the nervous system? In this connection, Joynson quotes Sherrington who, as a physiologist, was particularly interested in what he called the *integrative action* of the nervous system: '... it is nervous reaction which *par excellence* integrates [the animal], welds it together from its components and constitutes from a mere collection of organs an animal individual' (1947:2). Thus placing emphasis upon the behaviour of the whole individual does not seem to be good enough to distinguish psychology from physiology or neurophysiology. Especially when psychologists such as Zangwill suggest that 'the aim of psychology is to establish a system of general laws covering the whole field of higher nervous activity' (1967:294), the distinction between psychology and neurophysiology collapses. And, says Joynson quoting Scriven (1964:168), the belief that the future of psychology lies in neurophysiology is futile, for 'it is a future which lies after the grave, since that stage is no longer psychology.'

The situation thus leads to what Harré (1971) has called 'Joynson's dilemma': 'the only possible theoretical basis for the explanation of human behaviour is to be found in the physiology of the brain and central nervous system, and the adoption of this basis necessarily leads to the disappearance of psychology as an independent science.' But, says Joynson (1972), 'it is the doctrine of objective experiment which is impaled upon "Joynson's dilemma". I am not.' It is that doctrine which has to go, Joynson feels, and psychologists have once again to become students of mental life, merging philosophical with empirical investigations. And this indeed is just what we shall do in the latter part of this book. However, till then, there is still much to be learned from a further discussion of developments within the more traditional spheres of psychology. What of the prospects for physiological psychology (see A2)?

Problems and progress in physiological psychology: Weiskrantz

In spite of the problems Joynson discusses in his critique, modern behaviourists now assert that we must construct theories about events that go on within the skull. Indeed, they suggest that an increasing number of workers are turning to this approach, notwithstanding its difficulties, because 'they find it even more frustrating to try to understand how we tick by alternative routes' (Weiskrantz, 1973:516). And, interestingly enough, exponents of this approach are just as critical as I have been (but for different reasons) of the undisciplined theorizing of those who try to 'model' the mechanisms said to underlie behaviour. 'It is not that any of the models necessarily gives the wrong predictions', says Weiskrantz (1973:513), 'It is merely that none has the correct logical structure – the real nervous system is simply not put together in the way suggested by the models.' For instance, the real nervous system, suggests Weiskrantz, uses a form of 'coding' in visual perception that is not a spatial to temporal transformation, i.e. it is not a simple transformation of spatial patterns in the world into temporal ones in the brain, or vice versa (see A4).

How do we know this? On the basis of research by Hubel and Wiesel (1962) and Campbell *et al.* (1969), Weiskrantz replies. We discovered the complexity of the 'coding' process by delving into the nervous system itself; without such research we could not have discovered its complex nature. But is this true? Weiskrantz's own arguments can be used to show that it is not. He says (Weiskrantz, 1973:513):

If models are in danger of being cast-offs if they ignore

47

physiology, a study of physiology is also in a weak position.... [For] even when the physiologist knows in rough terms what functional category his observations are relevant to, there is a difficulty in knowing whether they are either necessary or sufficient for the function in question without studying the creature as a whole. For example, let us turn to the question of pattern discrimination once again. The feature detectors that have been isolated so far in the mammalian visual cortex are tuned to edges and lines of a particular orientation (Hubel and Wiesel, 1962). The discovery of these properties of cells in the visual cortex is one of the exciting breakthroughs of modern physiology. But they are patently insufficient to account for the properties of pattern vision, because *we can recognize patterns independently of their orientation, within wide limits, and independently of their size as well*. Whenever a pattern is rotated an entirely new set of units is stimulated, and yet *we do not see a new pattern*. Hence some additional mechanism is required, and *it is the behaviour of the whole animal that tells us that it is necessary* and suggests to us, if we are fortunate, what sort of mechanism to look for. [My emphasis]

In other words, Weiskrantz could be heard as saying here that the fundamental facts which any neurophysiological account of vision must explain are the facts *we all know to be true* regarding our own visual abilities. It is these facts to which Weiskrantz refers and which, if they were thoroughly elucidated (which they are not), would set the goals of neurophysiological research. Now this is undoubtedly true and unexceptionable. But this is not to say, as Weiskrantz does right at the beginning of his article on problems and progress in physiological psychology, that neurophysiology is more fundamental than psychology in the sense that other types of explanation 'ultimately will be accounted for in terms of it' (p. 511). It is simply to say that theorizing in neurophysiological research is to be disciplined in the same way as I have already suggested for theorizing in psychological research:

by ultimate reference to what we all do in fact already know about ourselves. Regarding the nature of possible spatial–temporal transforms in the nervous system, consideration of the fact, for instance, that we all may visually survey a scene with quite different patterns of eye movement, yet all still see the same scene, should surely be sufficient in itself to call the idea of simple linear transforms into question.

Where does this all leave us as far as psychological research into pattern vision is concerned? Much work (Gombrich, 1960; Gregory, 1970), as well as reference to our own experience, shows that we can 'see' the same situation in quite a number of different ways. Psychologically, the task in pattern vision research is to discover why, of all the possible ways in which we might view a scene, we view it in the way that we do; in Gregory's terms, 'how do we arrive at the "object hypotheses" we use, and how do we choose between them?' Now I shall argue later that, as viewing a situation in one way rather than another is something that 'we' as agents do rather than having it done for us by our nervous systems, the reasons for it can be discovered in our actions – it is a matter not so much of the structure of our nervous systems, but of what we are trying to do, and what we or our ancestors have done in the past.

Now, presumably, having a nervous system is indeed a necessary condition of us being able to see anything at all, but, as Weiskrantz himself points out, it may not in itself be a sufficient condition. Only if in fact we try to 'see' things, and submit ourselves to a course of instruction by those who can already 'see' them, might it be possible for us to come to see the world as they do. I shall discuss this possibility of being instructed into ways of going on, in general, later. In pattern vision, it would constitute a form of research that made no reference to neurophysiology at all; it would instead be concerned with studying the exchanges between people responsible for the development of their perceptions. It is surely only in giving the physiological reasons for abnormal functioning that neurophysiological research on the normal, everyday functioning of our nervous systems comes into its

49

own. For the purposes of disciplining research in psychology, knowledge of our nervous systems is not necessary: knowledge of our reasons for acting as we do is.

We cannot expect Weiskrantz to agree with this conclusion, and to be fair I must point out that I did say after quoting him only that he 'could be heard as saying' that our knowledge of ourselves was fundamental: Weiskrantz himself ends by suggesting that 'it is the behaviour of the whole animal that tells us that it is necessary'. He, clearly, would at least tend to suggest that observational rather than experiential criteria were required. However, we must add here that, once again, this is the stock requirement of wholeness which has always given psychology such difficulty.

The need for an organizing principle: Dewey

So, powerful though Weiskrantz's arguments may be against those like Broadbent (1958), who build what he calls 'structural models', he still faces the task of integrating all the submechanisms he explores into a coherent mechanistic unity of behaviour (and experience). And it is not at all clear how he is going to satisfy this demand for unity. In this respect, as I pointed out earlier, psychology has been in a perpetual state of crisis: it has been unable to find theoretical entities or principles which can express the required unity – because, I shall argue, instead of formulating for itself a proper concept of organic forms, it has always attempted to assimilate all its studies to mechanical concepts. Thus each new 'atom', each new proposal aimed at achieving unification, leads in the end to an aggregate of fragmented parts.

In noting psychology's lack of an 'organizing principle' and in commenting upon the crisis as it then existed, John Dewey (1896) admitted that 'the idea of the reflex arc has ... come nearer to meeting this demand ... than any other single concept.' But he still felt bound to criticize it, not

... to make a plea for the principles of explanation and

classification which the reflex arc idea has replaced; but, on the contrary, to urge that they are not sufficiently displaced, and that in the idea of the sensorimotor circuit conceptions of the nature of sensation and action derived from the nominally displaced psychology are still in control.

Having said this much, Dewey then proceeds to criticize 'the nominally displaced psychology' and to offer his alternative in terms still valid today.

This paper of Dewey's, although difficult, is a classic, and I shall draw upon it in two ways: (1) to introduce a discussion of organic concepts to contrast with mechanical ones; and (2) to introduce the idea of a kind of knowledge which informs action, knowledge of values and meanings in contrast to our usual idea of knowledge being of objective things. I shall suggest that objective knowledge is the kind of knowledge we have only when we are withdrawn from action and merely contemplating or observing the world; knowledge in action is not objective knowledge at all.

Now what are the nominally displaced notions to which Dewey objects? The first aspect of it he discusses is manifested in our tendency, when attempting to explain anything, of analysing it into its parts and classifying them as if they could all exist independently and in isolation from one another. Dewey says:

Instead of interpreting the character of sensation, idea and action from their place and function in the sensorimotor circuit, we still incline to interpret the latter from our preconceived and preformulated ideas of rigid distinctions between sensations, thought, and acts. The sensory stimulus is one thing, the central activity, standing for the idea, is another thing, and the motor discharge, standing for the act proper, is a third. As a result, the reflex arc is not a comprehensive, or organic unity, but a patchwork of disjoined parts, a mechanical conjunction of unallied processes.

This tendency to analyse behaviour into a sequence of separate events is, of course, still with us. In discussing recent developments in 'Cognitive psychology', Broadbent (1971: 193) remarks:

> Throughout these various fields there are a number of recurrent strands of thought. One of these is the separation of the processes between S and R into successive stages: the detection of features of S, followed by the selection of some features, followed by a transformation or encoding of them, followed by a choice of action, and so on ... and the stage is arrived at which a search for their physiological basis may be reasonable.

But it is just the very separation of the process in the way that Broadbent thinks valuable that destroys, Dewey suggests, the organic unity of behaviour.

Before turning to a more detailed discussion of Dewey's alternative to the analytic approach, let me make some general comments about our knowledge of mechanical and organic structures: mechanical assemblages are constructed piece by piece from objective parts – that is, from parts that retain their character irrespective of their context of existence, irrespective of whether they constitute a part of the assemblage or not. Organic structures, however, are not constructed piece by piece – on the contrary, they grow. Furthermore, unlike objective mechanisms, they only exist (live) in a state of exchange with their surroundings. In the course of such exchanges, they transform themselves from simple individuals into richly structured ones in such a way that their 'parts' at any one moment in time owe not just their character but their very existence, both to one another and to their relation to the 'parts' of the system at some earlier point in time. As well as existing in space they are qualitatively transformed through time, thus the history of their structural transformations is just as important as the logic of their momentary structure. It is the possibility that organic structures may qualitatively transform themselves that Dewey finds important, so let us now return to his account.

If we take a relatively complex piece of behaviour – Dewey takes the example of the child reaching for a candle and being burned, discussed by William James (1890) – and follow standard analytic practice in studying it, we would first analyse it into a sequence of isolated events: first the child would be thought of as experiencing a sensation of light, which would be a stimulus for the grasping following it as a response; and, in turn, the burn would be thought of as a stimulus, which is followed by the withdrawing of the hand as a response, and so on. As a result of a response, one stimulus situation is replaced by quite another. If this were really the case, Dewey points out, there could be no unity of experience at all, only a sequence of disconnected jerks, the character or significance of each jerk having to be defined objectively, in isolation from the act as a whole within which it plays its part. As a mechanical assemblage, the reflex arc fails in the very purpose for which it was introduced: it describes a merely contingent collection, a set of events that just happen to have occurred together, rather than a set with a unified structure, experienced as a complete act.

As an alternative, Dewey suggests that in reality there is no sequence of separate events in organic activity at all; what happens in an organism is more like a redistribution of tensions, a transformation of its structure; and it is this transformation that determines the quality of what is experienced. In the case of the child, then, its activity should not be thought of as beginning with a stimulus event, but with a transformation, with what Dewey calls a 'sensorimotor coordination'. We should begin with the movements of the child's body, head, eye muscles, etc., in relation to the light. Such a 'coordination' produces a transformation or redistribution of previously existing tensions. In other words, the real beginning is not with an external event, but, Dewey says, with an 'act of seeing', and it is the sensation resulting from the act that gives it its value or significance – simply, the value of an act is a function of its consequence. If this redistribution of tensions, this qualitative transformation in the structure of the organism motivates, next, an act of reaching, then both seeing and reaching can be considered as constitutive parts of some larger whole. But, again, the larger whole is not an act of seeing

53

followed by an act of reaching, for both seeing and reaching continue throughout the act. We have, says Dewey, an act of seeing no less than before, but one now transformed and enlarged as an act of seeing-for-reaching-purposes. There is still a sensorimotor coordination, but one with a transformed structure and thus a transformed value to it. It is not a matter of substituting one thing for another – what is seen in the act of seeing is only completed when the act of reaching is also completed, for as we said, it is seeing-for-reaching-purposes. 'The fact is,' says Dewey, 'that stimulus and response are not distinctions of existence, but teleological distinctions; that is, distinctions of function, or part played, with reference to reaching or maintaining an end.'

Thus the behaviour of organisms is not for Dewey a sequence of objective events: it is an act. It is something an organism as an agency does, without it, like a machine, being caused to do it by external events. As an agency, an organism acts not, like a machine, blindly, according to predetermined principles, but as a being that can continually modify and adjust its own activity in relation, not only to its circumstances, but also to its own needs and interests. And while what it does may be structured into a whole hierarchy of subordinate acts, what it does is nonetheless still, overall, an act – the organism undergoing continuous qualitative transformations of its structure.

We thus mislead ourselves in thinking about the behaviour of organisms in two ways, if we assimilate them to the classical, natural scientific framework: (1) we do not treat organisms as agents able themselves to do things – thus we continually search, mistakenly, for the external *causes* of what they do; and (2), by applying in an unwarranted fashion, Dewey claims, the serial way of proceeding which we do follow in our more deliberately planned activities – in which we first do A, and then do B, and then do C, and so on – we search, mistakenly, for the separate units in all organic activity, in which there is in reality a continual merging of one phase of the activity with another. This latter is an example of what he calls the 'psychological or historical fallacy', in which 'a state of things

54

characterizing an outcome is regarded as a true description of the events which lead up to this outcome.' The fallacy is the common one of describing processes solely in terms of their products, of saying in perception, for instance, that a process which eventuates in the seeing of objects is simply 'seeing objects'. In the child/candle example here, Dewey would suggest that the child does not at first see that there is 'a candle' before him, and that the seeing of this object (while at first it may cause reaching movements), as a result of the experience of being burnt, causes avoidance movements. Such an account would be quite mistaken, he would say. For Dewey, the child first has to learn what kind of stimulus it is that confronts him, he has to learn its value or meaning. In this learning, the child himself has to coordinate the seeing phase of his activity with its manipulatory phase. As a result, he can learn, among other things, that it is a light-which-if-touched-will-burn-him; but that is, of course, just one small part of learning what it is that confronts him; that, for instance, it is something adults call 'a candle'. His learning of what kind of stimulus it is, is then an outcome of a process, an act which he as an agent performs. In general, we determine what a stimulus situation is for us by the way we act towards it, the response we make to it, and both stimulus and response are known to us after the event, in a retrospective evaluation of the completed act when we reflect upon it. Further discussion of the action of agents is now best postponed until the more systematic treatment in Chapter 6. For the moment there is still more worth saying about the problems of integration and fragmentation in the standard classical approach.

Unlike objective phenomena, organic phenomena give rise to parts which are perceptually distinguishable but not physically separable. In analysing them we use, as Dewey puts it, not 'distinctions of existence' but 'teleological distinctions': thus their 'parts' are known for what they are, not in terms of their shape or any of their other formal characteristics, but in terms of the part they play in relation to all the other parts constituting the whole. For instance, as a partial analogy, we may note that in the game of chess, as long as the pieces can be distinguished and placed in proper relation to one another at the beginning of the game, their shape is irrelevant. They are known for what they are – 'pawn', 'king', etc. – in terms of the part they play in the game, the part determined by the rules. Just as sounds in a language, their shape is irrelevant as they are 'reciprocally determined', not objectively but by their function in relation to others in a system. The analogy is only partial, though, for in organic wholes the parts not only owe their character to one another, they also owe their existence to one another.

Now it is clearly tempting, lacking any clear 'picture' of organic structures (because they exist both in space and through time), to assimilate them to ones which we can picture, to assume in fact that they are like mechanisms which can be studied by the classical analytic method of taking parts in isolation from one another. But separating organic 'parts' from one another destroys just that precise set of mutual influences by which the 'parts' of a living system all determine one another's functioning. The classical analytic method, while appropriate to mechanisms, destroys organisms irretrievably; it is appropriate to the products or outcomes of productive or formative processes, but not to the study of the processes themselves. Like the actions of agents, further discussion of the formative processes of organisms will be reserved for later chapters.

'Cognitive psychology' and the limits of mechanism: Neisser

I began, in this critical commentary on the current state of the art in the science of behaviour, by discussing physiological psychology, in deference to its claims to be drawing support from those frustrated by the lack of success of other approaches. But surely, notwithstanding Weiskrantz's claims, many feel that 'cognitive psychology', with its structural models, is in fact still the standard bearer of those in the mainstream of current psychological research. It is thus that I now turn to a discussion of Neisser's (1967) *Cognitive Psychology*.

56

By the term 'cognitive psychology', Neisser means both an approach and a theory. In his approach he is not a simple *S-R* theorist, nor is he a physiological psychologist. While he has no doubt that both human behaviour and consciousness depend entirely on the brain in interaction with other physical systems, one will find little if any biochemistry or physiology in his book. 'The task of the psychologist trying to understand human cognition', he says (Neisser, 1967:6),

> is analogous to that of a man trying to discover how a computer has been programmed. In particular, if the program seems to store and reuse information, he would like to know by what 'routines' or 'procedures' this is done ... He wants to understand its utilization not its incarnation. [see A1]

There must be, Neisser assumes, a logic to the perceptual processes he discusses, there must be some rules, laws or principles which determine people's behaviour and which the behavioural scientist, in his investigations, can discover – it is this assumption that we shall ultimately question.

Now while Neisser is a behaviourist to the extent that he takes the standpoint of an external observer, and studies people's behaviour rather than their experience, he is not a simple connectionist like Watson. He begins his book by asserting that we have no immediate access to the world or to any of its properties; that whatever we know about reality has been mediated, not only by the organs of sense, but by complex systems which interpret and reinterpret sensory 'information'. He then goes on to show in what way the notion of 'information' plays a central role in his whole approach and is linked to his use of the 'program analogy'. He does so as follows: Neisser points out that Bartlett (1932) discussed ideas of cognitive transformations, memory schemata, and the like; but if memory consists of transformations, he asks, what is transformed? It is the *information* dealt with by something like a program controlled computer process that is transformed, Neisser replies; and it is the structured pattern of its transformations that he wants to describe. These are the principles of operation he wants to discuss.

That, then, is his approach. He wants to understand, as he puts it, 'how the mind works', and he wants to do it by discovering the logical structure of the 'information' which, like a program, controls its operation. As physiological considerations are only of peripheral interest to him, he claims his approach is essentially a psychological one. We shall have occasion to criticize every aspect of his approach (except his lack of interest in physiology). The views of an old and outdated philosophy condition its every aspect: (1) the use of experiments to confirm or refute abstract structural models, (2) the talk of mechanisms and the search for their principles of operation, (3) the idea that 'we' have no immediate access to reality, and (4) the idea that our knowledge of things is enshrined or encoded as 'information'.

The theory that Neisser proposes for the processes that mediate between 'us' and the world is that 'seeing, hearing, and remembering are all acts of *construction*, which make more or less use of stimulus information depending upon circumstances' (1967 : 10). His idea is that, in interpreting an input, one does not simply examine it and make a decision as to what it is: an appropriate schematic match for it is constructed, a 'theory' is formulated as to what it is, and sensory information is used merely as data in confirming or refuting its appropriateness. At least, this is what is supposed to happen in the second stage of the perceptual processes he outlines, for they are presumed to have two stages: the first is fast, crude and holistic, and (in computer terms) works in parallel – it consists of holistic operations which are supposed to form the uninterpreted units to which attention may then be directed in their interpretation. The second process is supposed to be deliberate, attentive and detailed, and works sequentially – it constructs the perceptual object in the process of interpretation using a technique which may be likened to 'analysis by synthesis' (a computer technique in which a pattern is identified in terms of the routine a computer must go through to construct a match for it). The first stage involves what Neisser calls 'preattentive processes', the second involves 'focal attention and figural synthesis'.

As a theory it has many attractive features, not least its emphasis upon active, form-producing processes – the formative powers of organisms will occupy our attention in later chapters. However, whilst we shall assume that people (unlike other organisms) can be agents in their own formative processes, modifying them as their own requirements and circumstances demand, Neisser assumes the processes to be automatic, mechanical ones – and he searches, of course, for their principles of operation. This, as we shall find, drives him into having to assume the existence of a homunculus, something like a little, disembodied being sitting in the central 'control room' of the organism, trying to decide which action to initiate on the basis of the information such processes give him.

As automatic, computer-like processes, human cognitive processes can be analysed, Neisser assumes, into sequences of objective events: first, holistic, 'preattentive processes' form the uninterpreted object, and then the constructive processes of 'focal attention', themselves sequential, form another object – the uninterpreted object becoming known in terms of the 'structured pattern' representing the transformations involved in creating a match for it. Thus, what is experienced by us as a meaningful whole, an act of perception in which we make an effort to see something, is broken down by Neisser into a sequence of events, each of which can occur automatically and in isolation from one another. Thus, even though there is a process of construction going on within us, 'we' are only ever given its product, and it is that which is responded to and remembered. For Neisser, 'we' are not there as agents in the conduct of these processes; seeing objects is not something that 'we' do, it is something that our cognitive processes do for us.

But more than this. The processes that Neisser discusses lack the motor phase of sensorimotor coordinations; they are simply acts of seeing, hearing and remembering. They lead, not to an understanding of the value or meaning of the stimulus in relation to a response (or action) that the organism is trying to complete, but merely to a view of what the stimulus is as

59

an object. This is knowledge of a kind only of use to those withdrawn from action, contemplating the world (perhaps with the purpose of planning some future action, looking at what there is, to see how it might be more suitably arranged). But, in action, one needs more than a plan of the situation one wants to attain; one needs to understand one's current situation too and to know its meaning, its 'symbolic' value, what it 'points to', what actions it 'allows'. If one is unable to understand the meaning of one's situation in this sense, it is difficult to see how one can decide what in particular to do to change it in the attempt to attain a more desirable situation in the future. In fact it is difficult to see how, in Neisser's account, the 'symbolic' value of things is coped with at all, for it is only their shape or form that is matched in the process of figural synthesis. And, as we have already seen, the 'symbolic' value of things has nothing to do with their shape or form; but it is to do with the parts they play in relation to the parts played by other things in constituting some larger whole. But the only kind of larger wholes in Neisser's objective account are mechanical assemblages.

The next thing is to say that, although Neisser talks of *acts*, and even (as we shall see in a moment) of *agents*, his acts of seeing, etc., are not in the end acts that 'I' do; they are acts done for me by my 'cognitive processes', the results of which 'I' as an agent may only 'utilize'. Later, in Chapter 6, I shall maintain that to the extent that seeing is an act of mine, something that 'I' do, then it is up to me how I do it. Thus it may not involve any processes essentially like the program-controlled processes of computers. Indeed, Weiskrantz's assertion that 'coding' in pattern perception is not a simple spatial–temporal transform would support the same view. If there are not any 'programmed' processes, however, then there is no work for Neisser's program analogy to do, for there are no program-like structures to be discovered. Neisser, however, while he does discuss the necessity of postulating an agent, does not allow us to be agents in our own perceptual and cognitive processes; Neisser gives the agent the job only of dealing with the results of an automatic information processing he presumes goes on within us. 'Unpalatable as such a notion may be, we can hardly avoid it altogether', he says:

> If we do *not* postulate some agent who selects and uses stored information, we must think of every response and every thought as just the momentary resultant of an interacting system, governed essentially by *laissez-faire* economics. (1967:293)

What Neisser is proposing then, he realizes, is a homunculus, situated within us somewhere, with, as he assumes at the outset, no immediate contact with reality. The notion *is* an unpalatable one. But it is just the impasse to which his approach – the classical scientific approach of testing abstract theories from the standpoint of a disinterested, disembodied, outside observer – leads; the need for a homunculus follows directly from it.

By searching first for mechanisms, Neisser postpones the crucial task of dealing with meanings. He is thus unable to give any account of when, where, why or how one particular 'mechanism' rather than another is used by an organism in the coordination of its behaviour with its circumstances and with other organisms. The really important processes psychologically, those to do with understanding and deciding, must be attributed to just that aspect of the whole mechanism thought to constitute the organism that has not yet been discovered: the central 'agent'. The best that Neisser can do in this respect is to hope that the 'executive routine' processes currently being developed in computers may help us to see our way out of the impasse. But in the end, not without a touch of sadness one feels, he leaves the issue on an equivocal note by saying, 'it is fair to say that no contemporary psychological theory and no existing program deals satisfactorily with the constructive nature of the higher mental processes' (1967:300).

And, we might add here, nor will they ever if they continue to base their approach on the computer analogy, for quite a number of reasons, some of which we have already discussed: (1) computers are not agents in the processes they execute; (2) they do not undergo qualitative transformations in their structure, neither do they grow their own structure; (3) they are not immersed in the world in the sense of living in a state of exchange with their surroundings; and (4) they have no social character in the sense of being able to help in the completion of one another's projects by understanding one another's goals. In short, compared with organisms, never mind persons, mechanisms are somewhat limited.

Why computers must have bodies in order to be intelligent: Dreyfus

Of the four reasons above why computers are an inadequate analogy of man (and *a fortiori*, of organisms) Dreyfus (1967) has discussed the first three. After pointing, like Dewey, to the classical but now outmoded philosophical assumptions that still control approaches to the study of cognitive functioning, Dreyfus turns to a phenomenological analysis of what people are in fact able to do; that is, he studies what appears to us to be the actual structure of our experience of ourselves. He discusses specifically: (*a*) the way in which we seem able to work through from a vague, global meaning in a situation to a more specific, detailed one, both in pattern recognition and problem-solving; and (*b*) how our experience of tool using differs from our experience of observing objects. I shall apply what Dreyfus has to say to the three issues mentioned above in turn.

(1) Embodied agents
In pattern recognition, Dreyfus begins by making the same point as Neisser, that in recognizing an object we at first give a global meaning to an otherwise indeterminate (but determinable) sensuous experience, and we then proceed to make this global meaning more determinate by further exploration. The process is thus one of moving from a sense of the whole to its parts, our sense of the whole determining the significance of the parts. Thus, 'in recognizing a melody, the notes get the values they have by being recognized as parts of the melody, rather than the melody's being built up out of independently recognized notes' (Dreyfus, 1967: 17). However, for Dreyfus,

the global meaning of a situation is given us directly from our immersion as embodied beings in the situation.

But it is the recognition of spoken language that offers the most striking demonstrations of this global character of our experience (see A7). Using such sentences as 'Rapid righting [which can, of course, be heard as "writing"] with his un-injured hand saved from loss the contents of the upturned canoe', Lashley (1951) demonstrated that one must take in a sentence as a whole – over a period of five seconds or so – before one can fully determine its meaning, as the end often influences the interpretation one must put upon the beginning. A grasp of the overall global meaning seems to determine the specific values to be assigned to the elements constituting it. Thus Dreyfus quotes Oettinger, a worker in the Harvard Computation Laboratory who attempted to apply the results of linguistic analyses to the mechanization of speech processes, as saying, 'perhaps ... in perception as well as in conscious scholarly analysis, the phoneme (the supposedly smallest sig-nificant element in speech sounds) comes after the fact, namely ... it is constructed, if at all, as a consequence of perception, not as a step in the process of perception itself' – the percep-tion of speech thus being conducted by quite some other means than in mechanical terms, i.e. than by building up wholes, piece by piece, from objective elements according to pre-established principles. And it is difficult to imagine how a computer, which must work on completely determinate data according to well-defined rules, could be reprogrammed to use an underdetermined expectation of a whole in order to determine the elements of that whole.

In problem solving, too, we must first move from a vague sense of confronting a problem to a clear definition of what the problem is – 'defining the problem' time and again being the major part of the problem solving process. Once a problem has been defined, then the kinds of 'mean–ends analyses' de-vised by Newell, Shaw and Simon (1959) may be carried out mechanically – that is, Dreyfus points out, as long as the possible ends constituting the problem, and the possible means for solving it have been introduced into the program by the programmers before the solution process is set in motion. In genuinely creative problem solving, however, we do not know what our end is until we have achieved it: a painter painting his picture must move forward and back, painting a bit then stepping back to sense the result, only finishing when he senses the painting complete. He does not know until he completes it, however, what the detailed constitution of his painting will be. Similarly with writing, the writer must both write and then read his compositions; and he too will not (as I shall not) know the final constitution of his book until he has finished it. One works from indeterminate intentions to their more determinate realization.

As a result of his analyses in these spheres, Dreyfus suggests, then, that what makes people different from computers is that not only do people as agents have a continual sense of their own functioning, but also as embodied beings they possess needs and interests in terms of which they structure their experience of their situation and their actions in it. Their embodied needs give them a sense of what is relevant and what is irrelevant. A machine, at best, can be set to attain a required 'target' state and, on the basis of objective information, compute whether it has attained that state or not. People, however, have a much more flexible criterion of whether they are fulfilling their own expectations. They need not keep stopping to check whether they are meeting certain objective requirements in their actions (although they may if necessary), for they are able to sense in the course of their activity whether, on the basis of their needs and interests, they are coping with their situation. Here 'coping' is defined not in terms of any specific characteristics, but in terms of how what they have done relates to their knowledge of what still needs to be done. Thus, whereas present computer programs call for a machine to recognize an object in order to decide how it should be manipulated, people may manipulate objects in order to recognize them, to recognize what they are in relation to their own needs and interests – Dewey also makes the same point in other terms. Such things as human needs and interests cannot be simulated by a digital computer whose only mode of existence is as a series of determinate states and which, like a disinterested, unconcerned, disembodied observer, has at best specific target forms rather than the fulfilment of needs at which to aim. Without this human form of information processing, says Dreyfus, which requires that we have bodies and be immersed in the world as agents possessing a continual sense of our own functioning, we would be unable to cope with the indefinite number of possibly relevant facts in the everyday world, or be able to solve ill-defined problems.

(2) *Structural extensions: tool using*

Since pattern recognition is a skill, and since our ability to discriminate relevant from irrelevant aspects of our situation depends upon their relation to our needs, the question of whether an artificial or mechanical intelligence is possible, suggests Dreyfus, boils down to whether there can be an artificial embodied agent. If such mechanisms are to be given a continual sense of their own functioning, what would be the nature of the knowledge of their own 'bodies' that they would require? We can approach this problem via a discussion of tool using.

Polanyi (1958) has argued that our knowledge of something as a tool is quite different from our knowledge of it as an object: we learn, for instance, about a hammer as an instrument while using it to knock in nails, but we learn about it as an object by examining it itself – by operating on it rather than with it. Or, again, the blind man using his stick does not discover the stick as an object in his investigations, but the objects that there are in the world around him. And similarly, just as we may know a hammer both as a tool and as an object, so we may know our own bodies in the same way: one finger may be used as an 'instrument' to explore another. We can direct it in such a way that the investigatory process in which it is involved eventuates in knowledge of the other finger as an object. Now knowledge of how to conduct such a process of investigation must be distinguished from the products of such processes (as Dewey has already suggested), thus touching is to be distinguished from the touched, seeing from the seen, speaking from the spoken, etc.... However, although productive processes are not to be characterized by their products, our knowledge of something as an instrument is only acquired in our attempts to form such products. We learn how to use it in relation to the products we have produced in using it; but the use to which we put it in the future is entirely up to us. Thus, although the structure of an instrument may limit the uses to which it can be put, it would be a mistake to think that its use was specified by its construction absolutely – and one may extend the analogy here to embrace the use of sentences (as instruments) to achieve ends in human affairs (Shotter, 1974a).

The situation here is the complement of one already discussed: in interpreting the meaning of one's situation, one has to appreciate what it indicates for one's conduct in the future. In any skill, one needs to understand how to use one's tools appropriately in relation to achieving one's goal: one needs to understand the meaning of what one is doing, the way that it relates to what has been done and what it indicates as remaining to be done. In talking, for instance, one needs to know how to use one's words as instruments in 'pointing to' one's goals. To do this, one needs a knowledge of words, not as objects, but as 'tools' – knowledge of quite another kind than objective knowledge.

For computers, there is only one kind of knowledge, one way to deal with 'information': it must be presented as an object for the processor. But, as Dreyfus points out, for an embodied agent there is a second possibility: he can build up skills and assimilate instruments as extensions to his body. Thus an embodied agent can dwell in the world in such a way that he need not know everything objectively in order to know how to act, since he is using things to satisfy his needs; he needs only knowledge of things as means not as ends.

(3) Immersion in the world

Finally we may remark that, as embodied agents immersed in the world, we cannot help but be in both continual and immediate contact with our surroundings in one way or another. Our sense of our situation may very well be vague and ill defined, but this is not to deny either its reality or its determinability.

The image of man that Dreyfus leads us to, then – in contrast to the discrete state, precise, sequential operation, digital computer – is of a being of at least partially indeterminate structure, to a degree influenced by and to a degree influencing its surroundings, which develops in successive stages states of increasing refinement and detail. But Dreyfus has nothing to say in all of this about our relations to others; it is thus not surprising that he also has nothing to say about the idea of personal selves. While he is concerned with intelligent action, he is not so concerned with the socially responsible agent's task of acting intelligibly and responsibly. Dreyfus's men may be agents but they are not yet persons (see D1). We must, however, ourselves leave persons for discussion later.

The predicament of psychology

We began this chapter by asking what constituted the subject matter of psychology as the science of behaviour, for such a psychology has not found it easy to distinguish itself from other, closely related disciplines. While other sciences may deal with part functions, it was felt that the science of behaviour should, in some way, deal with the whole animal. But, as we have seen, what constitutes the character of wholeness associated with organic phenomena has, so far, eluded those who, in pursuing the classical, natural scientific approach, feel driven to assimilate organic to mechanical forms of order. The notion of mechanical assemblages, constructed precisely, piece by piece, from objective parts, fails to capture the idea of somewhat structurally indeterminate, growing and developing organisms; since, at any moment, there is always more of such structures to come, they are, in a sense, essentially incomplete.

As classical scientists, methodologically, psychologists have taken the standpoint of external, detached and disinterested (disembodied) observers, viewing people's behaviour merely as a sequence of objective events – rather than, as in everyday life, being involved in exchanges with other people, appreciating the meaning of what they are doing. And theoretically, psychologists have treated people as machines, searching for their parts and the principles by which such parts operate, automatically, to produce the behaviour observed – rather than, again as in everyday life, assuming that others like themselves may be agents in their own actions, acting in a skilled manner as integrated individuals in relation to needs and interests. In taking only an observer's standpoint, they attempt to understand human behaviour using only observational or behavioural criteria – rather than taking into account any experiential criteria to do with what only we know about our own behaviour. Concerned only with the outside form of behaviour, it is not difficult for such psychologists to argue that all behaviour – mechanical, organic or personal – can be 'seen as' having the same kind of structure to it, a mechanical form. Thus, rather than modelling behavioural processes organically and treating behaviour as a continuous sequence of irreversible, qualitative transformations, each one bringing a new set of distinguishable but inseparable elements into existence, they model behaviour mechanically and treat it as if it were a disconnected series of episodes, each one being seen as a reversible change in the configuration of some basic set of elements, all of which can be known for what they are in isolation from one another.

But this is not all; we have yet to mention what is perhaps the greatest defect of the classical approach: as natural scientists we psychologists attempt to discover the nature of things independently of any responsibility that we might have for their behaviour; we want to understand the nature of things in themselves, objectively. When we turn this endeavour round upon ourselves, when we attempt to discover our own nature independently of any responsibility that we might have here for our own behaviour, the result is absurd. We discover exactly the opposite of what we really want to know. In our study of ourselves we want to understand in what way we can be responsible for our own behaviour. This, not the discovery of 'principles of behaviour', should be, I shall argue, the task of psychological research. Rather than mere behaviour, responsible action should be the problematic of psychology. However, as Sedgwick (1974) pointed out, a problematic goes together with a perspective within which it can be viewed and with paradigms by which it can be investigated. In setting out a new task for psychology, it will also be necessary to set out a new perspective – an indeterministic, temporal one to replace the timeless, deterministic one of the classical approach – and new research paradigms – involving exchanges between people rather than disinterested observation of their behaviour, exchanges concerned with discovering their reasons for action rather than with discovering their inner workings.

In its one hundred years of existence, psychology has changed a great deal without changing at all. In declaring its independence of philosophical investigations, and thus suspending all further analysis of its fundamental assumptions, it rendered itself totally dependent upon the philosophical assumptions (about the nature of the world, people, and the doing of science) which were current at the time. 'Psychology is thus', says Koch (1964:5), 'in the unenviable position of standing on foundations which began to be vacated by philosophy almost as soon as the former had borrowed them. The paradox is now compounded: philosophy, and more generally, the methodology of science are beginning to stand on foundations that only psychology could render secure.' For we need to understand how we understand; the doing of science is itself a human activity and as such an understanding of its conduct is one of the psychologist's tasks. Psychology's failure to conduct itself in a reflexive manner and to construct its own foundations (Shotter, 1970a) is made even more intense by the current need for its success. I cannot resist ending this chapter by quoting Koch's (1964:5–6) account of the predicament of psychology:

There is a strange circularity, then, in the predicament of

psychology. Psychology has long been hamstrung by an inadequate conception of the nature of knowledge, one not of its own making. A world now in motion towards a more adequate conception begins to perceive that only psychology can implement it. Yet psychology is prevented from doing so because, almost alone in the scholarly community, it remains in the grip of the old conception. But this state of affairs could lead to a happy consequence: should psychology break out of the circle just described, it could at one and the same time assume leadership in pressing toward a resolution of the central intellectual problem of our time and liberate itself for the engagement of bypassed, but important and intensely interesting, ranges of its own subject matter. Moreover, it can find courage to do these things in the circumstance that the very sources upon which it has most leaned for authority – physics and the philosophy of science – are, together with the rest of the scholarly community, urgently inviting them to be done.

The prospect then is an exciting one. In the next chapter I want to go more deeply into the origins of the 'old conception' that currently grips psychology, and gripped it in Dewey's day too. I want to do this because, if we can establish that such a conception did not come into our world from natural necessity, but from human choice, and that its fundamental character is speculative rather than factual, then we might raise even more the courage to change it for a new one. So, perhaps, *reculer pour mieux sauter*, we will turn next to the history of the classical approach, to motivate intellectually the construction of the alternative I shall begin to describe in Chapter 6.

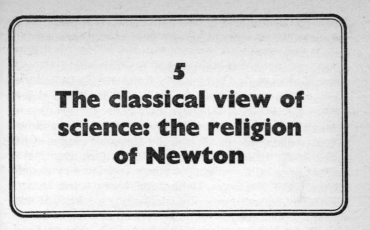

5
The classical view of science: the religion of Newton

For some long time now, psychology, thinking it could be a science simply by using what could be described as the methods of science, has attempted to exist as an autonomous discipline with a monopoly on 'the facts' as to man's essential psychological nature. It has asserted that the true facts about human nature can only be established by objective experimentation and other associated techniques, and it has taken as its task that of establishing how people, as mechanisms, actually 'work'.

Society and social science

Now it would be wrong to argue that the development of this aim in psychology was a product of purely internal factors, that only rational considerations within the discipline led to the adoption of one image of man rather than another. There were external considerations also. Humanistic images of man were proposed in the Renaissance but, as we have seen (in Chapter 1), there has been a gradual tendency in the period since from humanism to naturalism, to a demotion of man from a player on the stage to a seat in the audience. The social context has clearly favoured one over the other (Gross,

1974), the mechanistic conception of man as a fixed, social atom over the humanistic one of him as a being able to transform himself. Why?

We may hazard the guess that a progressive society is clearly a changing society, one in which the social order is forever unsettled and unsettling. And that in such a society a desire for change is countered by a desire for stability, or at least by a desire for controlled change within an established system, avoiding the psychologically disturbing change of the system itself. Thus it is not surprising to find, even at the very inception of the progressive changes produced by modern science under Descartes, Galileo and Newton, the attempt to stabilize the social order by constructing a science of man with the explicit purpose of social control. Hobbes, as he said himself, 'occasioned by the disorders of the present time', suggested in 1651 that 'he who is to govern a whole nation, must read in himself, not this or that particular man; but mankind'. But how was mankind in general to be known? If 'life is nothing but a motion of the limbs', said Hobbes, our hope would seem to lie in applying the science of Galileo and Newton to human affairs. And a line can be traced from Saint-Simon with his Religion of Newton, followed by his pupil Auguste Comte with his positivist social physics in France, from Jeremy Bentham with his Utilitarianism and James Mill with his mental chemistry in England, through to the behavioural scientists of our day. Their hope of plotting men's social 'orbits' as one can plot planets' orbits remains unchanged to the present day. 'Perhaps the greatest social contribution that can be made by specifying man in the same terms as machines', says Dawson (1974:262), 'is that by doing so we can scientifically control man within his environment so that it and man are mutually enhanced' – the 'we' being left here carefully unspecified.

Saint-Simon failed to establish his Religion of Newton, and Jeremy Bentham's Felicific Calculus (a kind of arithmetic of pleasure meant to help in controlling fairly the distribution of happiness) still remains to be invented. But even now, when doubt about this whole approach is widespread, and humanistic attitudes are in revolt against naturalistic ones, there are still those who are vigorously reasserting that this is indeed psychology's proper approach. Thus Brand (1971:312) says, 'Psychology's task is surely to specify the kinds of mechanisms involved in generating acts of all kinds', or its task is to ask questions such as 'What kind of mechanism makes such an achievement as perception possible?' However, as even those with ambitions to control behaviour are forced to admit, it is still an ambition rather than a reality; this approach has yet to fulfil its promise. And as there are good reasons why, I think, it never will, it is worthwhile going into its character more deeply in order to find out where its essential inadequacies lie and to provide points at which to contrast it with an alternative.

Behind appearances

We must begin by thinking about the very fundamental biases and presuppositions in the classical approach. To do this, we must go back to Greek thought. Plato suggested that truth was not to be found in mere appearance but behind or underlying it. In his allegory of the cave, he likened men to prisoners in the cave, chained so that all they can see is the wall in front of them. Behind them is a fire. On the wall they see shadows of all kinds of things which, although they cannot turn round to discover this, are in fact carried by bearers between them and the fire. Miraculously, a man escapes. First he spends some time wandering in the cave, in the world of particular things, discovering the causes of the shadows. But later he discovers the mouth of the cave and emerges into the sunlight. At first he is dazzled, but gradually he comes to see the true reality of things. He returns, as a philosopher, to instruct those who remain as prisoners seeing only the shadows in the true forms lying behind the appearances. He does not, of course, have an easy task, but he must persist.

What we have here then is the idea that Plato expounded elsewhere also, that the ever changing flux of experience can

73

only be interpreted in relation to a knowledge of some unchanging forms against which the raw data of sense are judged by the mind. These are, Plato suggested, Ideal Forms, which are the real forms behind appearances.

Established here, then, is a bias in favour of searching for the *ideals* underlying the changing flux of experience, as only these are thought to give us knowledge of reality – rather than the *flux* itself being thought of as constituting in itself a real influence upon us; there is also a bias in favour of dealing with *forms* – rather than with *meanings*; and, further, there is a bias in favour of what could truthfully be *said* – rather than upon what could be appropriately *done*. All these taken together suggest that theoretical knowledge should have primacy over practical knowledge, a bias which is still with us today.

Galileo, Descartes, Newton and Laplace

Given these biases, it is not surprising to find Galileo, under the influence of the renaissance of Greek ideas, writing in his great polemical work of 1629, *The Assayer*:

> Philosophy is written in this great book, the universe, which stands continually open to our gaze. But the book cannot be understood unless one first learns to comprehend the language and read the letters in which it is composed. It is written in the language of mathematics, and its characters are triangles, circles, and other geometrical figures without which it is humanly impossible to understand a single word of it; without these one wanders about in a dark labyrinth.

For Galileo, the language of nature is not assimilated in infancy in the course of everyday exchanges with one's world and other people; it is a special language of Ideal Forms, almost like a foreign language, which must be learnt formally, in schools, before one can study nature. It belongs, in other words, not to the world of everyday life, but to a secondary, painfully constructed, idealized world, a product of the con-

74

templative world of scholarship which few of us inhabit – those of us, most of us, who lack it can only wander in a dark labyrinth. The influence of Plato's thought here is clear, the dark labyrinth replacing the cave.

But is this true? Are those of us who have failed to learn mathematical codes blind to nature and to one another? Is there not a mother tongue of nature, so to speak, which we all learn in childhood, and which provides the ground for learning secondary, more formal and reflective modes of thought and expression, such as mathematics, afterwards (see C2)? I shall want to suggest that there is an intersubjectively valid 'everyday life' world for people, which they acquire knowledge of in the course of their everyday exchanges with one another, and from which the more 'objective' world of science is abstracted, and that this 'common sense' world is irreplaceable!

However, for the last 350 years, part of that everyday life world has been for us the intellectual framework of modern, objective thought; we have learnt how to 'dwell in' it and to 'see' reality in its terms. But more than this we now live in an all but man-made environment of triangles, circles and other rational forms. It is thus no wonder that nature has come to mean for us Galilean nature, and that in taking the 'natural' attitude the modern framework provides, the full character of our everyday life world is ignored.

In saying this, though, we must not mislead ourselves into thinking that our ancestors were stupidly ignorant and blind. The Galilean/Cartesian conception of the world clearly exerted a powerful influence. Descartes's great belief, set out in his *Discourse on Method* in 1637, that it was indeed possible to translate, methodically, all that was unknown into the realm of indisputable common knowledge, vitalized our modern age. His method was to start from 'clear and distinct ideas' and to proceed by way of those 'long chains of reasonings, quite simple and easy, which geometers are accustomed to using to teach their most difficult demonstrations'. Via the unity of mathematics – remember that Descartes had shown how in coordinate geometry, geometry could be expressed in algebraic terms – such a method promised a unified view of the cosmos. For the nature of the world is such that with this method, Descartes said, 'there can be nothing so distant that one does not reach it eventually, or so hidden that one cannot discover it'. It is, he felt, a world in which all that there is of it is already in existence; our uncertainty about it is a mere matter of human ignorance, a situation which can be remedied if only we can discover the appropriate method for doing so.

When we speak of the method of the natural sciences, we can thus trace at least part of it back to Descartes's *Discourse*. It was to this that Newton added the experimental method, asserting that one should proceed from data obtained in experiments to theories, rather than beginning with theories. In a letter to the secretary of the Royal Society of 1672 he wrote:

> The best and safest method of philosophizing seems to be, first, to inquire diligently into the properties of things and to establish these properties by experiments, and to proceed later to hypotheses for the explanation of things themselves. For hypothesis ought only to be applied in the explanation of the properties of things, and not made use of in determining them.

But actually it was only possible for Newton to assert this given the way in which Descartes had idealized the subject matter of his natural philosophy – hypotheses did enter into the determination of 'things'. Descartes (in a letter to his publisher) describes his idealization of the world thus:

> I resolved ... to speak only of what would happen in *a new world*, if God were to create, somewhere in imaginary space, *enough matter to compose it*, and if he were to agitate diversely and confusedly the *different parts* of this matter, so that he created a chaos as *disordered* as the poets could ever imagine, and then afterwards did no more than to lend his *usual preserving action* to nature, and let her act according to his *established laws*. [My emphases]

76

I have emphasized all the assumptions Descartes makes in setting out his idealization of our world. It is, of course, an entirely speculative picture. But it is from this that the modern natural sciences emerged. Scientists are told that they must study the abstract stuff, matter, which is to be known in terms of its measurable properties, *spatial extent* and *motion*, and whose behaviour is to be investigated to yield God's established laws. All 'things' in the world, except, Descartes thought, men's rational souls, could be brought into the confines of such an investigation, as they could all be treated as identical in terms of the motion of matter moving according to mathematical laws. This set the scientific task for the next three and a half centuries.

Viewing the world in such colourless terms fell in with what was another of Galileo's requirements: the demand that science concern itself only with what John Locke was later to call primary (objective) qualities, and that it ignore secondary (subjective) ones. To understand what Galileo meant by this, let me quote another famous passage from *The Assayer*:

Now I say that whenever I conceive any material or corporeal substance, I immediately feel the need to think of it as bounded, and as having this or that shape; as being large or small in relation to other things, and in some specific place at any given time; as being in motion or at rest; as touching or not touching some other body; and as being one in number, or few, or many. From these conditions I cannot separate such a substance by any strength of my imagination. But that it must be white or red, bitter or sweet, noisy or silent, and of sweet or foul odour, my mind does not feel compelled to bring in as necessary accompaniments. Without the senses as our guides, reason or imagination unaided would probably never arrive at qualities like these. Hence I think that tastes, odours, colours and so on are no more than mere names so far as the object in which we place them is concerned, *and that they reside only in consciousness*. Hence, *if the living creatures were removed*, all these qualities would be wiped away and annihilated.

But since we have imposed upon them special names, distinct from those of other and *real* qualities mentioned previously, we wish to believe that they really exist as actually different from those. [My emphases]

But are not tastes, odours, colours and so on real determinants in how we act in the world? Galileo's world is for us a world 'out there', the 'external' world which is outside our agency but yields to our manipulations. It is the objective world of science from which 'all living creatures have been removed'; it is a world without conscious or self-conscious beings. But surely, it is not that world, but our world, the world in which we live and of which we are a part, that we are now as psychologists trying to understand. And this is a world in which tastes, etc., in which intersubjective understandings, residing only in our consciousness, play a real part in determining what happens. Such shared understandings are not just idiosyncratic phantasms, they are a real part of our everyday life world, and as such just as much a real determinant in what we do as other, so called, more objective determinants.

This then, is, the Galilean/Cartesian world. It is a world that must be investigated for the laws regulating the motions of its objective parts; investigated, that is, in such a way that what is observed is observed independently of any supposedly subjective characteristics of the observer. It is an all-already-existing world in which the only changes are changes of re-arrangement. Nothing in it passes into existence or out of it again. If we are unable to predict our future in such a world at this moment, that is not because it is in principle impossible – on the contrary, it is because we are still too ignorant; we have not yet amassed enough knowledge; yet more research is needed. In such a world, as Laplace (1886) realized:

An intellect which at a given instant knew all the forces acting in nature, and the position of all things of which the world consists – supposing the said intellect were vast enough to subject these data to analysis – would embrace in the same formula the motions of the greatest bodies in the universe and those of the slightest atoms; nothing

78

would be uncertain for it, and the future, like the past, would be present to its eyes.

It is thus a world in which the future is merely hidden like the distant regions of space (indeed time in it is spatialized); and it seems possible, ultimately, to know everything!

Such hopes and beliefs as these still motivate, I feel, much of what is called scientific psychology today.... It is surely possible, isn't it, to discover completely how man works? Well, it may not be.

It is from these attitudes, then, that modern science emerged: from the belief that our only contact with reality is mediated via spoken truths (or encoded information) about the Ideal Forms 'behind appearance', to Descartes's belief that reality was best conceived of as consisting of separable parts in motion according to pre-established laws. What also emerged, quite unavoidably, were all the problems we still have with our fragmented and lifeless self-images.

But note, Descartes said 'I resolved to speak ...'; he chose to think about the world in that way. Galileo and Newton too. The forebears of modern science could only, however, make proposals and suggestions; they did not, one day, just find themselves driven of natural necessity to act as they did. They invented their own way of going on, and the power of their inventions is a measure of their genius. But we are not of necessity bound to follow them. It is only because we choose to believe, mistakenly, that we are entities constructed piece by piece from separable parts, like machines, that we adopt and expect to be effective the current analytic and reductive modes of self-investigation. Within this classical framework, there is no other task to which the scientific psychologist could address himself than that of searching for the 'mechanisms' underlying behavioural appearances.

I shall show how this view can be criticized in the next chapter. The approach I shall use will perhaps by now be already obvious. I shall argue that it is not because we are made of atoms and molecules moving according to natural laws that we can think and act intelligibly and responsibly in the world; it is only because we can think and act intelligibly and responsibly in the world that we have been able to devise ways of dealing with the material world as if it were made of what we call 'atoms' and 'molecules'. For we must remember that the doing of physics is itself a human activity, and its concepts and its findings emerge from and return to their source in what people do in the world. And that when we talk about (our) atoms and molecules moving according to natural laws, we are talking about what we mean by the expressions 'atoms', 'molecules' and 'natural laws'. It will soon be one of our tasks to criticize (at least what psychologists take to be) the physicists' view of the natural world (physicists themselves began to question the classical conception long ago), for, as psychologists, we need a far richer conception: one in which it is possible for people to hold and share *beliefs*, to execute *intentions*, and to give one another *reasons* for their actions. This, however, is to anticipate what is to come. I would like to end this chapter by showing how psychology, in attempting to be a natural science, has been more true to this classical conception of the natural world and the thinking man's task in it, than it has been to the nature of man.

The task of the scientific psychologist

While Miller may extol the virtues of attempting to understand (and predict) behaviour instead of attempting to control it, the fact remains that the experimental method is concerned with attaining control, not understandings.

Above we have reviewed most of the assumptions it makes before it begins any of its investigations; and it is clear that they constitute a large and coherent body of belief that has informed and structured all our work in the natural sciences until very recently. Thus we can appreciate why, no matter how one might try to conduct one's psychology – as an introspectionist, S–R behaviourist, physiological psychologist, cognitive theorist, etc. – if one attempts to conduct one's activity as a natural scientist one always ends by searching for the 'mechanisms behind appearances', and contributing to the control of behaviour. No alternatives are available; it is no wonder that one always finds the 'nominally displaced psychology still in control'.

Attempts to question this attitude in the past have met with contempt. Hull dismissed as a 'defeatist attitude', a 'doctrine of despair' (1943:26), the idea that human behaviour could not be reduced in all cases to automatic, mechanical processes, identical for men and animals. Thus he entitled his major work simply *Principles of Behaviour* (Hull, 1943), 'on the assumption that all behaviour, individual and social, moral and immoral, normal and psychopathic, is generated from the same primary laws' (1943:v). For Hull, 'progress in this new era will consist in the laborious writing down, one by one, of hundreds of equations; in the experimental determination, one by one, of hundreds of empirical constants contained in the equations; etc., etc.' (1943:400). The point of all this being, of course, 'the satisfaction of creating a new and better world, one in which, among other things, there will be a really effective and universal moral education' (1943:401). Just how hundreds of equations, specifying hundreds of principles of behaviour, will in fact bring about a better life is left unspecified. But one cannot resist remembering here Plato's urging in the *Republic*, that the philosopher, having grasped the Ideal Forms behind appearances, should return from his place in the sun to rule as king over those still in the darkness, if there is to be any real justice among them.

Hull did not succeed in writing out his hundreds of equations. However, whereas Hull attempted to elaborate a 'hypothetico-deductive' and hence predictive science of behaviour as a preliminary to control, Skinner – who has clearly succeeded Hull as the most influential of the explicit behaviourists – has devoted himself directly to the problem of controlling behaviour. Like Hull, concerned not with helping us to understand what we are and what we might be, Skinner is also a philosopher king at heart, concerned with discovering how we all should live. And even before his now notorious *Beyond Freedom and Dignity* (1972), he was telling us in his

Science and Human Behaviour (1953) that not only was an applied science of behaviour feasible, but that salvation by science was perhaps our only hope for the future. But, and this is most important, 'if we are to enjoy the advantages of science in the field of human affairs, we must be prepared to adopt the working model of behaviour to which such a science will inevitably lead', he says (Skinner, 1953:5). And we need not guess at what this model may be, for Skinner (1953:447) tells us:

> The hypothesis that man is not free is essential to the application of scientific method to the study of human behaviour. The free inner man who is held responsible for the behaviour of the external biological organism is only a pre-scientific substitute for the kinds of causes which are discovered in the course of a scientific analysis. All these alternative causes lie outside the individual.... These are the things which make the individual behave as he does. For them he is not responsible, and for them it is useless to praise or blame him.

And, again, we find that the point of Skinner's prescriptions for the conduct of a science of behaviour is that the principles it produces should be applied in the construction of a culture, a new culture, designed by experts, to replace our old, deteriorating one.

Well, we all desire a better world, now perhaps more than at any other time in the immediate past. But is it either psychology's task or prerogative to provide it? Let me end this chapter by returning once again to Miller's (1969) wise comments upon these issues.

He notes that if one does take psychology's task to be that of directly promoting human welfare, then, 'in difficult cases where disagreement is most probable, something that advances the welfare of one group may disadvantage another group. The problem is to decide whose welfare we wish to promote' (p. 1064). And the trouble is, of course, that due to the general indeterminacy of human affairs, it is impossible to form any clear concept of what is good for us in advance of

82

trying things out in practice. Thus, Miller concludes (which will perhaps seem incredible to many) that psychologists should not aim directly at promoting human welfare at all, but at promoting psychology. 'It is our science', he says (p. 1065), 'that provides our real means for promoting human welfare'. That is, one must add, if it can be made a science adequate to man in general rather than at present adequate only to those who seek to control the behaviour of others.

Miller proposes that, instead of control, psychology should exist for the purpose of understanding ourselves, whatever our natures may be. If it did, then, instead of embarking upon journeys with unknown destinations, seeking the means to live in ways that experts like Skinner can only guess will be better for us, we could first seek to understand how in fact we do live, and what in fact we are. And if, as Miller suggests, psychologists could succeed in 'giving away' psychology, we could all then decide which of all the possibilities of self-change before us we would seek the means to realize. Deciding what, in practice, we should all do is not the psychologist's task – not as a psychologist, that is; his task is to help say what in theory we might do (but as a person among the others with whom he shares his life he has, presumably, as much right to argue his preference as the rest).

The picture above is a naive one, but I hope that it is at least clear that it is a quite different account of how psychology might function in human affairs than the one of it as an applied science of behaviour, providing technologies of behavioural control.

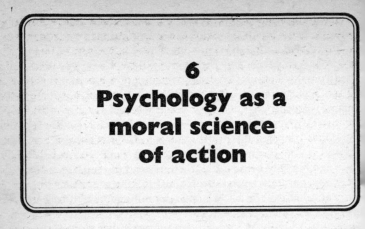

6
Psychology as a moral science of action

In this chapter I want to introduce, as an alternative to psychology as a natural science of behaviour, psychology as a *moral science of action*. That is, we will not conduct it as a science of events happening outside our agency of control, in which, as we have mentioned before, we attempt to discover the nature of things independently of any responsibility that we might have for their behaviour. It is to be a science in which we do try to understand the nature of the responsibility we can have for the behaviour of things, especially ourselves.

The inadequacy of observational criteria

The classical view may capture a large body of our significant experiences of what we call our 'external world' – that portion of the world which we do not inhabit as an agency but which may nonetheless be made to yield to our manipulations. However, it utterly fails to capture our experience of our own functioning in such a world. Because of this and what has now been shown to be the frankly speculative character of the 'old conception', I would like to suggest an alternative basis for our investigations in psychology: *a basis in the sense of responsibility which we all can have for our own actions*. On such a basis, psychology immediately becomes the study of action rather than behaviour, concerned with things people sense themselves as doing, rather than with observed patterns of movement said to be caused by external events. Let me make clear what I mean by this by showing in what way the study of behaviour is inadequate for the understanding of human affairs and people's actions.

If we take the view of external observers, as indeed we must in a classical natural science, we must regard man as a natural object differing only in complexity from other natural objects, his parts subject to the same laws and principles as those governing the rest of the material world. His behaviour is then constituted for us as a pattern of events (to the extent that we can perceive, classify and characterize it as a pattern, that is), and it is on the basis of this and this alone that we must decide what he is doing. But such external observations of men's behaviour must miss some crucial distinctions which men themselves can and do make in their own experience of what they do: we all distinguish, and indeed if we are to be accounted as persons by others we must be able to distinguish between that for which we as individual personalities are responsible and that which merely happens irrespective of our agency. In other words, we ourselves do not do all that we may be observed to do, and although this may be apparent to us it is not apparent to merely external observers (although it can be apparent, as we shall see, to those who more than merely observing involve themselves in exchanges with us). Instead, then, of taking the standpoint of the behaviourist, who, in just viewing people's activity from the outside, ignores the distinction they can make between what they as persons do and what merely happens irrespective of their agency, we must take a more personal standpoint. We must study what people themselves do rather than, so to speak, what their nervous systems or cognitive processes do for them.

The distinction I have been making above is the distinction between *actions* and *events*, *doings* and *happenings* which has been explored extensively of late in the philosophy of human action (R. Bernstein, 1972; Hampshire, 1959; Macmurray,

1957, 1961; Mischel, 1969; Peters, 1958; Taylor, 1966; Winch, 1958). It is a distinction that is certainly crucial in everyday life, where we are continually concerned with whether a person himself intended what he did or whether it happened by accident, or with what a person meant by his action. It is only because people themselves know whether they intended their activity or not, and whether they achieved what they meant to achieve, that they are able to answer such questions; beings unable to distinguish between what they intended and what just happened would find such questions quite senseless.

Besides being crucial in everyday life, though, such a distinction is crucial in the conduct of science, absolutely crucial: it is only because we can sense, when acting in accord with theories of what the world might be like, whether the results of our actions accord with or depart from the expectations engendered by the theories, that we can ever put such theories to empirical test – this is the only way of establishing the nature of a theory's purchase on reality. If people were unable to distinguish between what happened as a result of their intentional activity and what just happened, by itself, there would be no basis for scientific inquiries at all. Thus, no other more fundamental basis for deciding the truth of empirical matters exists; nor will one ever be found – not as some have proposed, in the organizational complexity of matter – for how could it ever be established as a true basis? Weiskrantz and other physiological psychologists may feel that, ultimately, self-conscious acts will be shown to be events determined in much more complex ways than other more mechanical activity, but they can only propose that as a theory needing empirical test. And any validity that such a hypothesis might have would still rest, like the validity of any other scientific hypothesis, upon our ability to recognize the consequences of our own actions. So, although we may feel that experimental methods function to establish the truth and nothing but the truth, we must realize that they do not establish the whole truth: they merely establish what we can and cannot expect to do on the basis of our theories, i.e. in terms of the way in which we 'see' or interpret the nature of the world around us. But there is more to our experience than we ever 'observe'.

Our sense of our own responsibility is, then, not only a central part of everyday life – it is at the very heart of science itself, and is quite irreplaceable. Scientists without any sense of their own functioning would be unable to do experiments.

Agency: I can move my finger

I take it then, that it is a fundamental fact of human life that, without quite knowing how it is that they can do it, people can themselves be responsible for at least some of the things they do. That is, no matter what metaphysical notions one may have (like Skinner) about everything being caused by other things external to them, the future being determined like the past, etc., people can (in an everyday sense of the word) cause at least some of their own motions.

I can move my finger. I can do it, without being caused by anything else to do it, for no other reason than just to demonstrate that 'I' can do it. Now, undoubtedly, a necessary condition of my being able to move it is that I possess the appropriate muscles and nerves, bone and brain, etc., and that furthermore, when I move it, they all work in an orderly and consistent fashion. Indeed, if they did not, how could I acquire any skills at anything and come confidently to expect to be able to express my intentions without being continually surprised at the result. For me to be free to act as I want, it is necessary for the behaviour of all my parts to be lawful. But the fact remains that it is not my muscles and nerves, etc., that cause me to move my finger: I do it.

Now it may seem strange to say this, but saying 'I' move my finger does not preclude the possibility of all my parts (right down to my atoms and molecules even) all working according to physical laws. In the past a mysterious chasm has separated our experience of ourselves from our knowledge of our bodies, a chasm that seemingly could not be bridged. Thus many, alive to the facts of physics on the one hand and to the facts of experience on the other, have felt driven to say, as Schrodinger (1967:93) does, that:

> The only possible inference ... is, I think, that I – I in the widest meaning of the word, that is to say, every conscious mind that has ever said or felt 'I' am the person, if any, who controls the 'motions of atoms' according to the Laws of Nature.

The mystical nature of this conclusion can be dispelled if one realizes, as we have already mentioned, that whenever we speak of atoms and of the laws of nature, we are speaking of what *we mean* by the expressions 'atoms' and 'laws of nature'. They are expressions associated with a particular way of 'seeing' the world and of manipulating it by the means it provides.

To repeat, physics is a human activity, and its concepts and its results emerge from and return to their source in what people do in the world. We can conceive of and manipulate the world as if it consisted only of atoms and molecules moving according to laws just because we are free to act in accord with our theories and can be responsible for what we do. And one thing we can do, as an intrinsic part of the whole natural scientific method, is to abstract the 'physical world' from the world of agents with their capacity to interfere in the operation of otherwise automatic processes, i.e. remove, in theory at least, all living creatures. We ourselves have, however, surreptitiously crept back in again and, not knowing how to 'see' ourselves in our scientific view of things, find our own presence sometimes bewildering. Thus, for instance, we find Heisenberg (1958:15) commenting: '... the objective reality of the elementary particles has been strangely dispersed, not into the fog of some new ill-defined or still unexplained conception of reality, but into the transparent clarity of a mathematics that no longer describes the behaviour of the elementary particles *but only our knowledge of this behaviour*.' [My emphasis] And he continues by reminding us, as I have been trying to do in this chapter so far, that 'science always presupposes the existence of man and we ... must remember that we are not merely observers but also actors on the stage of life'. The conduct of physics has become, at least for Heisenberg, something of a psychological problem – and it is to issues such as this that Koch alludes when he suggests that psychology should take the lead in pressing towards resolution of the problems besetting all the sciences.

The world outside ourselves has, seemingly, orderly processes within it which will continue to repeat themselves without any help from us. But the discovery, identification and characterization of such processes is, it seems, up to us. And the prize of our discovery is that we might be, in Descartes's words, 'masters and possessors of nature'; while the risk, as the Faustian myths express it, might be that in the process we will lose some precious part of ourselves. But it is, after all, 'we' who conduct the process; and we are not of necessity bound to continue in the future as we have done in the past. We can be agents in our own processes.

Later I shall suggest that in general men experience life as a task, and that while they may be born living, to survive they must try to survive. For men, it is not something that happens automatically; they have to intend it, and the quality of their trying determines the quality of their lives. But here I merely wish to point out that to act we must try to act, and the quality of one's effort (the character of one's intention) determines the quality of the result. Thus, for instance, to see one must try to see. We may, while lost in thought, appear to be staring at someone, and they respond accordingly. But we fail to notice, as we are intending some quite other result. Or, again, we may try to see the details in a scene, or go 'glassy eyed' and fail to interpret anything that lies before us, seeing it just as a mosaic of coloured patches – painting it as such, if we are an artist. We may try to see in many different ways. As scientists, we must of course try to see things objectively. And so on, and so on. In listening too, one must try to hear in order to hear, and what one does hear depends upon what one is trying to hear. Acts of seeing, acts of hearing, and acts of remembering too, are all things that I can make happen by trying to make them happen – they are not things that my 'cognitive processes' necessarily must do for me, the finished results of which 'I', as a homunculus, can only view and must accept as given.

More than trying, though, one must know how to try: one's actions must be informed with a knowledge of the situation in which one is placed and the kind of action required to modify it according to one's needs. In other words, there is a skill to be learnt, and one must acquire the appropriate knowledge as a basis for such a skill. Now, while the causes of one's actions may not be other actions, as the causes of events are other events, this does not mean to say that one's actions come out of nowhere, that they have no rational origins at all: they have reasons. They must be understood as attempts to achieve goals, to realize intentions. But more than this: in human affairs, they must be understood as attempts to realize intentions in a particular kind of way, a way that conforms to standards or criteria shared by all those within one's own community. Only by acting to conformity with such criteria can one coordinate one's activity with theirs. One has to learn how to try, then, in a way that makes sense to others. And, as Dreyfus points out, one only learns how to try in the process of trying; it is in the course of one's efforts to achieve the same goal (or what counts as the same goal) time and again that one's actions may be transformed from faltering, experimental and exploratory ones to smooth and skilfully executed actions. That is, again, if one makes the effort to effect such a transformation, for even the development of skills does not seem to happen automatically; someone (oneself or others) must intend such improvements in the performance of one's actions.

Constructive and responsible action

We have begun to paint a picture here then of man not as an impotent reactor, with his behaviour determined by his circumstances and his genes, but of him as an active agent able to make things happen, able to construct events.

Chein (1972) has discussed just such an image of man. For him, 'the essential psychological human quality is one of commitment to a developing and continuing set of unending, inter-locking, interdependent, and mutually modifying long range enterprises' (p. 289). In other words, we certainly live in relation to a set of organically (rather than mechanically) organized concerns. However, we do not live like animals who act as they must, as their own bodily states demand (at least, so those who theorize about animal behaviour tell us). Lacking any species-specific way of life, we live in relation to a set of concerns which, with the crucial help of its ancestors, our community has constructed for itself. Thus people's actions are not to be explained casually, as sequences of objective events linked by causal principles, but intentionally. That is, in general, people's actions are to be explained as attempts to help in the realization of projects, goals, enterprises or ideals which they have invented amongst themselves. And it is in this respect, its direction towards the realization of ends that do not yet exist, the way that it brings into existence things entirely new, that human action must be considered as essentially *constructive*.

No other beings appear to live in relation to such an inter-locking system of commitments which they have constructed for themselves like this; no other beings seem to have constructed (or invented) their own ways of life like this! And it is this, Chein feels, rather than our erect posture, the structure of our hands, our prolonged infancy, or even our language, that makes man unique: 'To the extent that a human organism (that is, a creature born of woman and sired by man) fails to develop such a commitment', he maintains, 'it is not yet fully human, though it may have the potentiality of becoming so' (p. 289). And it is only communication in relation to such a system of commitments, he argues, that gives human language its peculiar nature. It is by the character of his concerns that man is to be known from the beasts: rather than a victim, man may be a master of his circumstances, acting to reconstruct them and in the process, in discovering how to live in his new circumstances, reconstructing himself.

Now acting in relation to such a set of commitments implies that the nature of man's awareness of his circumstances is of a different kind to that of animals. In acting, men show not just awareness of their physical circumstances, they also show awareness of their social circumstances. For they act not just in a manner appropriate to their immediate surroundings in a species-specific manner, but in terms of a particular relation they have momentarily assumed to all those with whom they share their lives. Thus they act self-consciously, in a knowledge of who and what they are, momentarily, in relation to others in their community (and who, in the past, have been in their community). Thus people do not, like animals, deal directly with nature; they deal with it indirectly, from known 'positions' within a culture, in terms of a knowledge of the part their action might play in maintaining or progressing the culture, no matter how vague, shallow or implicit this knowledge may be. Thus, even when 'I' alone am responsible for what 'I' do, I owe my knowledge of what I can do to my relations with others.

Mead (1934) has discussed extensively the distinction between merely intelligent conduct on the part of animals and the socially responsible, and thus truly self-conscious conduct of men. While animals may respond to one another's actions, it is, for Mead, being able to respond to our own actions in the same way as others respond to them (respond reflexively, that is), that makes men's actions self-conscious. 'The apparatus of reason would not be complete', Mead (1934:138) suggests:

> unless ... the individual brought himself into the same experiential field as that of the other individual selves in relation to whom he acts in any given social situation. Reason cannot become impersonal unless it takes an objective, non-affective attitude toward itself; otherwise we have just consciousness, not *self*-consciousness. And it is necessary to rational conduct that the individual ... should become an object to himself.

To plan what he might do in the future, a person must be

able, in theory at least, to place himself, just as much as other things, in positions other than that he currently occupies. The self must be, as Mead is fond of saying, something that can be 'an object to itself'. It has a strange dual nature, as both agent and other in action, and subject and object in thought – it is, after all, a reflexive term. And Mead continues by describing the situation in which such a condition arises:

> ... one may hear without listening; one may see many things that he does not realize; do many things that he is not really aware of. But it is where one does respond to that which he addresses to another and where that response of his own becomes a part of his conduct, where he not only hears himself but responds to himself, talks and replies to himself as truly as the other person replies to him, that we have behaviour in which individuals become objects to themselves. (1934: 139)

In such circumstances, people are not reliant upon others to react to what they do in order, then, themselves to have something upon which to base their next response. They are able to plan, execute and understand the meaning of long sequences of their own activity all alone.

We shall return to a fuller discussion of Mead and his theory of the nature of the *self* later. The discussion above will be sufficient if it has served just to introduce the possibility that man's self-conscious activity – activity in which he himself knows what he is doing, even if it is as trivial as his moving his finger – is activity of an inherently social kind.

Causes versus reasons for action in the explanation of people's activity

I hope that enough has been said already to make it clear that in talking about action we are talking about something quite different from behaviour: the difference, let me repeat, is not to be found in observational criteria but in experiental ones; to outsiders action does not 'look' any different from behaviour. But we know that there are some things we do, while other things seem merely to happen, 'outside' our agency. Actions are done by people; events just happen.

Now we say that events that follow in an orderly manner from other events are the effects of causes: events that just happen are to be explained, then, by discovering their causes – or, more accurately, the causal principles thought to link them to other events (the 'established laws' thought to govern the happening of things in the Cartesian conception of the world). People's actions, however, are not to be explained by discovering their causes, for they are, after all, not events but actions; they must be explained by discovering the reasons people have for doing them. But here we must go carefully, for the term is somewhat ambiguous: in asking the reason for a person's action we may want (1) to know *what* it is he is (or might be) trying to do – the 'might be' here being most important as we shall see in a moment – and/or (2) to know *why* such efforts are valued. So when we ask 'Why did so and so act as he did?' we may be given a *technical* answer, being told the nature of the goal he is aiming at; and/or, given that we already know it, we may be told his *evaluation* of it, the place such a goal occupies in relation to all the other possible goals he might have tried to realize in the situation but did not. Thus those we question may in this case reply, 'he did it because it was easiest ... because he desired riches rather than rags ... because it was socially appropriate ... etc.'

I point out the evaluative aspect of reasons for action here only because in the rest of what follows I want to concern myself with the technical aspect, and we must avoid confusing the two. We shall return, but briefly, to the evaluation of ends later. Rather than what should be done, I want to consider now explanations of how things can be done.

Now to assert that people's actions are to be explained best by giving their reasons – to say, for instance, that the explanation of me putting these blocks of baked clay on top of one another is that I'm trying to build a house – is to assert nothing new at all. It is merely to describe the way in which we ordinarily, in everyday life, explain people's activity. And this may very well seem to many of you – especially those of you who as natural scientists dream of seeing into the inner 'workings' of things – a counsel of despair. It seems ridiculous to suggest that we should turn away from the study of 'cognitive mechanisms', the neurophysiology of the brain and sensory processes, biochemistry, etc., in our attempts in psychology to find the 'real' reasons for what we do, and that we should seek an understanding of it in the same way as laymen, using the everyday notion of 'reasons for action' as he does. But if we are to explain what people themselves do – their actions – then I think we must. So let me now try to show that the ordinary, everyday concept of *reasons for action* is a much more complex affair than one might at first suppose.

The transformation of spontaneous into deliberate action

I want to discuss in this section what I feel is the whole point of psychology as a moral science of action: the extension of our ability to decide for ourselves how we will act by making clear to us the nature of the goals available to us, so that we may choose what to do next. In other words, its concern is with how we may come to decide for ourselves what to do rather than merely acting as the situation requires: to act deliberately rather than spontaneously.

To begin with, however, let me point out that while knowing people's reasons for action may not help us with respect to the natural scientific goals of making formal predictions and achieving mechanical control – aims which are in any case of a dubious nature in human affairs – they may enable us to do many things at a practical level which otherwise we would be unable to do. For instance, very simply, finding another man's motions unintelligible, there is little we can do but stand aside, or intervene physically. However, on learning his reasons for action, on learning what he is trying to do (and there are many ways of doing that besides being told), one may try to help or hinder him as the case may be, by coordinating one's behaviour with his in a meaningful fashion.

Psychologically, however, the most interesting and important sphere we must consider is that in which deliberate action emerges – action for which 'I' alone can be responsible. And implicitly here we shall be discussing the transition from conscious to self-conscious activity mentioned in an earlier section. Being able to deliberate before one acts (or in the course of a complex action), and, as a result, make clear to oneself one's own reasons for action, is part of what it is to be an autonomous, responsible person, not reliant like a child upon others to complete and give meaning to one's acts. Those who can deliberate know, at least up to a point, what they are trying to do (and often also, why) – I say 'at least up to a point' here with good reason, for clearly more extensive reasons for people's actions may always be sought, and seeking them is the nature of our problem here. It is with these more extensive reasons that we shall concern ourselves in a moment.

In spontaneous actions, we do not decide what we are going to try to make happen before we act, we just act 'naturally', we say; we act spontaneously, in the course of events as required. In talking, for instance, we do not deliberate on which of all the possible speech sounds we might make is the next one we are actually going to try to make. We just talk without thinking about such things, and make the sounds as required, spontaneously, in the course of expressing our meanings (see A6).

Now the thesis that I want to discuss in connection with the emergence of deliberate action is drawn from Vygotsky (1962) – as, indeed, is the distinction between deliberate and spontaneous action itself: a person's spontaneous actions may be transformed into deliberate ones as a result of instruction by another person. And what is communicated from the instructor to the pupil is, I suggest, some *reasons* for the pupil's activity; he is instructed in the goals he might achieve by the movements he makes – a simple enough thesis, but one with important consequences.

Let me give you some examples of it in action. When I am speaking, I move my mouth (and the rest of my vocal tract) in certain ways. I do it. I am an agent in the process, not a spectator at a process done for me by my physiology. How it is that I can speak as I do, I don't know. However, if I want to make speech noises deliberately, not just in the normal course of speaking, then I need to know how to 'direct' my articulatory apparatus appropriately. At the most elementary level, the process is best described, I think, in terms of the vocal tract configurations at which I seem to be aiming while talking, i.e. the shapes we try to make with our mouths, where we put our tongue, etc. The work of the people at the Haskins Laboratory, New York (Liberman *et al.*, 1967), has provided us with a great deal of knowledge of these articulatory 'targets'. We are not aware of trying to make such shapes while speaking; we do not, as a matter of fact, deliberate in the process on which of all the possible targets we are going to aim at next. Yet this is certainly a way of describing what we could be trying to do in our talking, as if such an aim were the reason for us talking as we do. And knowing how to aim at such shapes would enable us to make particular speech sounds, not spontaneously as circumstances require, but deliberately as we require.

At a more overall level, when it comes to matters of sentence structure, there are again ways of describing what it is that we might be trying to do in our talk. The rules that Chomsky (1965) has adduced should, I suggest, be thought of as characterizing syntactic 'targets' at which we could be said to be aiming in our talk. Now, whether as a matter of fact we do, is beside the point here, for once in possession of such rules we may construct grammatical sentences deliberately and intellectually, referring to the explicit rules, whereas before we could only do it intuitively, without any good reason for saying why what we had just uttered was in fact a sentence.

So here, an account of what we 'might be' trying to do while talking, an account of some of the aims we might entertain, can be used, not to understand what underlies our talk, but to *overlay* it. So that, while talking, we may consciously and deliberately refer to the standards such rules provide if we require extra guidance in structuring the form of our expressions – as perhaps we do when writing, or in talking

97

totally 'out of our heads', using an elaborated code (Bernstein, 1972). Thus, it may very well be true, as Dreyfus points out, that the elements and principles we arrive at as a result of our scholarly analyses of language can only be constructed as a consequence of being able to talk, and are not necessarily a part of the process, which is in fact conducted by quite other means. Nevertheless, the fact remains that if we can indeed extract from our everyday practices a theory of those practices, that theory may be reflectively applied in deciding what to try to do next.

Ryle (1949:30–1) comments upon the relation between theory and practice thus:

> Rules of correct reasoning were first extracted by Aristotle, yet man knew how to avoid and detect fallacies before they learned his lessons, just as man since Aristotle, and including Aristotle, ordinarily conduct their arguments without making any initial reference to his formulae. They do not plan their arguments before constructing them. Indeed if they had to plan what to think before thinking it they would never think at all; for this planning would itself be unplanned.
>
> Efficient practice precedes the theory of it. . . .

And whether such theories of our practices account for what is 'really' the case is, as I have said, beside the point. It may very well be the case, as Dreyfus puts it, that '. . . although science requires that skilled performance be described according to rules, these rules need in no way be involved in producing the performance' (p. 29). Once produced, however, such rules may be referred to as a basis for deciding what to try to do next. Otherwise spontaneous performances may be given an intellectual basis, and people, even when acting quite alone, may then refer to it to evaluate their actions in terms of their significance to others.

Let me give another example of Vygotsky's thesis in action, one more obviously related to the function of *instructive social exchanges* in the development of deliberate action: a mother facing the task of teaching her infant (of, say, ten to twelve months old) to put shapes into a formboard must, I suggest, communicate to him the reasons for such action, i.e. what it is that he must try to do in such a situation if he is to act in a way which makes sense to others.

On first encountering the board, the infant may do all sorts of things with the pieces: chew them, throw them about, bang them or scrub them on the board, and so on. Occasionally, he may be observed to fit a piece into a hole on the board spontaneously. This, however, is not good enough for his mother. She will not be satisfied until it seems to her that he can do it deliberately. And she judges whether he is doing that by 'analysing' his concepts just as we have proposed concepts should be analysed: in terms of their implications. He must give indications in his actions that he did something as a result of *trying* to do it, that he *chose* to act that way rather than in some other way, and that he has some *reasons* for his choices – i.e. his performance is based on some knowledge of the situation. This is the result the mother must aim for in her exchanges with her child.

The topic is one of great research interest at the moment (Schaffer, 1974; Trevarthan, 1974). What some workers have proposed (Newson and Shotter, 1974; Ryan, 1974), to mention briefly the process by which reasons for action may be communicated, is that mothers act in such social exchanges as 'double agents': they act both on their own behalf and on their infant's behalf in giving the exchanges meaningful structure.

At first an infant has little power to satisfy his own needs. To the extent that a mother can interpret her infant's behaviour as having an 'intention' to it, she attempts to complete its 'intention' for him, and 'negotiate' with him a satisfaction of his needs, i.e. she tries to do what makes him, as she feels, happy. But the mother also has her own goals in such exchanges: she wants her baby to suck, to stop crying, to grasp her finger, etc., and in the context of the formboard to learn the activity she requires. She seems to do this by acting in response to his actions in such a way as to make what he does on the formboard instrumental in him maintaining his social contact with her – drawing on what seems to be a fundamental, inborn need in humans, the need for communication. She interprets and responds to his activity as if his intention had been something to do with fitting the pieces in, even though clearly it could not have been – there being no way of telling him, among all the kinds of other things he could do with the pieces, what he ought to do with them. As a result of her help, the way in which she completes the realization of what 'might be' his intention, his actions become incorporated into a circle of reciprocal exchanges between them. And to the extent that he learns to do that which maintains his contact with her (she having arranged it so), he comes to act in a way that at least makes sense to her – the child himself not being able to give an account till later of what it is that he is actually doing, simply learning first the practice of it. And thus the process continues, with the child being helped by his mother to a retrospective evaluation of his own activity; having performed a movement, it is given a social function by his mother.

Now it is not so much in this process that he learns new movements that he has never made before, but that he learns a meaning or a social use for movements that he can make any time. It is the mother's task to respond to what he does in such a way as to give his actions meaning. This is why the process just described bears no relation to operant conditioning, in which the frequency of a response, a movement, is manipulated as a function of reinforcement. Such a process has nothing to do with the learning of meanings, of reasons for action. In learning the appropriate reasons for action, the child learns how to act deliberately, as he chooses, not merely to act as required, under 'stimulus control'.

Vygotsky (1966:43–4) comments on the process thus:

> ... *we become ourselves through others*, and this rule applies not only to the personality as a whole, but also to the history of every individual function. ... The personality becomes for itself what it is in itself through what it is for others. ... The means of influencing oneself is originally a means of influencing others. ... We might (thus) formulate the general genetic law of cultural development as follows: *any function in the child's cultural development appears on the stage twice, on two planes, first on the social plane and then on the psychological*, first among people as an *intermental category* and then within the child as *an intramental category*.

Before anything becomes a mental function proper, located 'within' an individual, it must first exist externally, as an exchange between two people. We become ourselves through others. And the reasons why we become what we are can be found 'out there' in the world, rather than deep within our private, inner workings.

Reasons for action in the structure and history of our cultures

In detailed studies of actual situations like that above we can discover the immediate reasons for the mother's actions. However, different mothers have different styles, different ways of approaching the problem, and we must go beyond the situation under study if we are to seek more general reasons for the mother's way of going on. Does she, for instance, believe that her child ought to be learning how to do things on his own, or should he learn only to do as he is told and to rely always upon the guidance of others? Does she, perhaps, believe that the world is an essentially intelligible place that her child can learn to master or does she believe it to be essentially mysterious, such that the best he can do is to learn to protect himself against it? And so on. On the basis of very fundamental attitudes to the world, people do all sorts of things quite spontaneously, without deliberating upon them

101

at all; their actions have, nonetheless, a characteristic structure, informed as they are by such beliefs. To understand people's different overall styles, we must elucidate these beliefs. How can this be done?

One way of discovering some such possible beliefs is by interrogating ourselves – we are, after all, members of the same culture, sharing at least some fundamental reasons for action. We must conduct some conceptual analyses upon ourselves. Now, as we pointed out in our earlier discussion, this is not a matter of merely introspecting to discover the nature of our bodily 'feels': we face the task of discovering our own reasons for action. However, as our reasons for action are not something we necessarily think about before we act (and, indeed, we may avoid ever considering them, preferring to leave them in our 'Freudian unconscious'), we must discover them by the process already described in Chapter 3: just as in the investigations of natural phenomena, we must construct theories. And just as natural scientific theories must be tested, so our theories must be tested, not by investigating them for their empirical consequences, though, but for their conceptual implications. Thus, for instance, we may feel that a piece of behaviour we have observed was something a person did 'by accident', and we say so to someone else (a behaviourist, perhaps). He asks us our reasons. In an attempt to give him an answer we do not introspect our feelings, we point out that a part of what it is to do something accidentally is to be taken by surprise at the result of one's activity, that one denies responsibility for what happens, that one searches for other causes, that this and more is implied in the concept of 'accidental' doings, and that this is what was indeed observed to happen in this case. The behaviourist replies, of course, that it is all just behaviour, and that it all must have an underlying mechanical cause. And there the matter rests for him. But for us it does not. We must realize that there is a conceptual rather than a logical relation, a meaningful rather than a formal link between our theories and their implications, and that there are good reasons to be discovered which relate what men do now with what they have already done.

But such analyses of the immediate situation can only be carried so far, and, of course, one always wants to go further to even more general reasons for one's conduct. For instance, one may find in oneself, as I certainly do, that the reason for much of what one does in life comes from an interest in progress: it expresses itself in me as the need to discover how to do something tomorrow that I cannot do today. But if history books are to be believed, this was not a general reason for action in medieval times, only in modern times did men's actions become informed by it. To understand the deeper reasons why I act as I do, I must study the history of my culture to discover the genesis of this reason (and, in the study of mother–child exchanges, we can investigate its transmission); I cannot discover the reasons for its coming into existence in any form of self-interrogation. The 'pre-established' nature of cultures is discussed by Berger and Luckman (1967:77–8):

> An institutional world is experienced as an objective reality. It has a history which antedates the individual's birth and is not accessible to his biographical recollection. It was there before he was born, and it will be there after his death. This history itself, as the tradition of the existing institutions, has the character of objective reality.... Since institutions exist as external reality, the individual must 'go out' and learn about them, just as he must learn about nature. This remains true even though the social world, as a humanly produced reality, is potentially understandable, in a way not possible in the case of the natural world.

So besides being trained in finding within themselves and in the exchanges of others immediate reasons for action, students of psychology as a moral science must also undertake cultural and historical studies in their attempts to discover deeper reasons for these immediate reasons.

And the aim of all this, let me repeat, is not as in psychology as a natural science – to discover the underlying causes of our movements when we are not responsible for what happens – it is to discover reasons for what we already do but do spontaneously as circumstances require, so that as a result we may come to do it deliberately as we require. That is, so we might understand how to extend our responsibility for our own behaviour. It is thus quite appropriate, with such an aim as this, to designate this kind of science a *moral* science.

Psychology as a moral science of action rather than a natural science of behaviour can be seen, then, as having (1) a clear subject matter, (2) clear aims, and (3) clear methods of investigation, which, like those in the natural sciences, proceed by the construction and testing of publicly sharable, or intersubjectively valid accounts. In spite of this, it may still seem to some, as it does not involve work in laboratories with microelectrodes and electronic counters and timers, to be nothing but an 'armchair' activity. Well, that is as may be. But, as I shall make more clear before this book comes to an end, it cannot be conducted by those who do nothing but inhabit armchairs (or laboratories): as its aim is to help in continual modification and correction of our practices, it cannot be conducted by those with no experience of such practices. And, centrally concerned though it may be with beliefs, concepts and other essentially intersubjective things, its primary aim is not as in the natural sciences a theoretical one (to produce the one true account of how it all is for all time). Theories take on only a secondary importance within it as 'tools' to be taken up, modified, or put down as appropriate – as Popper (Magee, 1973) has advocated for all the sciences.

The task then is not so much to add to our knowledge of ourselves by thinking or seeing what has not been thought or seen before, but by doing what has not been done before – always remembering, though, that if what one does is to be intelligent, intelligible and responsible, it must be done in a knowledge of one's relation to one's community and its history. It is in action not thought that we discover and add to what we are. And psychology as a moral science of action, though it is not an 'applied psychology', is nonetheless essentially concerned with practicalities.

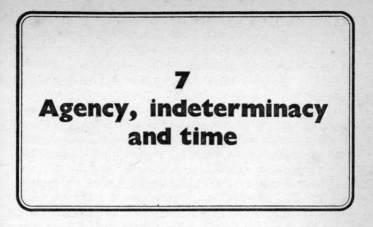

7
Agency, indeterminacy and time

In the last chapter action was discussed as the *problematic* in a psychology conceived of as a moral science; also discussed were *paradigms* of social exchange within which it may be studied. Now I would like to discuss a *perspective* within which the action of agents can be seen as a real possibility. For within the classical, deterministic scheme of things the idea of an agent being able to do things is inconceivable.

'Inside' and 'outside' us

We have taken it to be a fundamental fact that people can, without being caused by 'external' events, be themselves responsible for at least some of their own movements. We can say that it is 'within' their agency to control themselves so. For this to be possible the world must be a very different place from that pictured by Descartes as consisting of elementary particles in blind but lawful motion – the 'picture' to which behavioural scientists think all our motions must be reduced. Within this classical, deterministic, billiard ball universe, there is no way in which any processes could go on within a particular segment independently of any external influences upon it. In other words, a self-acting billiard ball would not just be surprising, it would be inconceivable in principle: activity intrinsic to an organized and self-organizing system, activity formed from within by a 'mentality', can be no different within such a perspective from external, mechanical motion.

However, for us in everyday life, there does seem to be a real distinction between what goes on 'inside' us and 'outside' us. Evidently, there are events happening in the world 'outside' our agency to control. But a part of what it is to say that a man is an agent is to say that as such, 'within' the particular region of physical reality he occupies as an agent, he can make at least some events occur independently of those which occur 'outside' that segment. In other words, if there are to be agents in the world, then it must be more of a 'loose jointed' place than the deterministic scheme allows. And the segments of reality agents occupy are not to be specified geographically, as particular locations in space, but by a quality of 'connectedness' between the events 'within' the segment not possessed by those 'outside' it. This has been discussed by William James (1890: 237): there is to our personal consciousness, he suggests, a 'sensible continuity'; that is, there is a sense of all the parts of our actions belonging together and being inwardly connected as parts of a common whole – the natural name for that common whole being, James states, 'myself, I, or me'. To say all this, though, about what is 'inside' and what is 'outside' us, is only to restate the fundamental distinction between actions and events, doings and happenings, introduced in the last chapter: without knowing how it is that we can do it, we can sense the difference between that for which we are responsible and that which merely happens, 'outside' our agency. And it is this that is fundamental for us.

The terms *inside* and *outside* are being used, then, with special meaning here – to make not a spatial but a mental distinction. Agents cannot be located like objects simply in space, for they manifest their character not just in space *but also through time*: hence, although 'within' us in the sense of belonging to us, our mentality is not necessarily something spatially confined within our bodies; agents may express their

106

mentalities out in the world in what, through time, they do there. The idea of an agency having events 'within' its control implies, then, not only a world of events much more loosely connected than those in the Cartesian/Laplacean world, in which all that happens in one moment is connected by an iron chain of causal necessity to what happens in the next, but also a world in which, through time, there is a continual passage from trying to doing, from possibilities to their realization. In other words, it must be a world in which at any one moment there are really alternative futures, so that what actually happens there depends upon what agents do.

Determining the future by our actions

I want to discuss in this chapter, then, an outline of an alternative to the Galilean/Cartesian/Newtonian/Laplacean conception of the world in which we live. In this classical conception, only one future state of affairs can succeed a particular present state of affairs; thus any genuinely constructive, creative and spontaneous events are inconceivable in principle. They would seem to have occurred without a cause at all, and that would be incompatible with the idea of a world operating according to established laws. Agents are thus unable to make anything happen in such a world.

But what if our belief in a predetermined future is mistaken? What if we are unable to predict the future in principle; not because we are ignorant, not because we have not yet done enough research, but because the future has not really been determined yet? What if we live, not in an all-already-existing world of inert matter in mechanical motion, but in a developing world in which things emerge into existence and pass out of it again, a world in which there are agencies with *powers* to make things happen (as Harré, 1970 suggests); a world in which irreversible and qualitative changes take place as well as reversible and quantitative ones; a world in which true novelties are possible?

Rather than denying ourselves any existence within our own

limited conceptions of the world, and insisting like Skinner that science is only possible if we continue to do so, we must invent a world in which it is possible for people to hold, share and act upon *beliefs,* to realize *intentions,* to have their actions informed by concepts, and to be able to give one another *reasons* for their actions; and in doing so help *transform* one another's mode of being in the world. We can only begin in this task as Descartes began, by examining what follows when we resolve to speak only of what would happen in a new world, somewhere in imaginary space (and time).

Indeterminacy

In building his new world, Descartes focused upon its *substance* and idealized it as particles of matter in lawful motion. We, however, will focus upon its *processes,* processes of action in which something is made to happen.

In acting we do something: using something as a tool or instrument we make something else, some material, take on a form different from the form it would have had if we had not acted. Thus, in acting, we determine at least some small aspect of the world. For this to be possible the world must be capable of being given a structure it does not already possess. That is, contrary to the classical Laplacean view, the world must be in some sense essentially *indeterminate.* If real human action is to be possible, the world cannot have an eternally fixed character, it must be a world that can be developed in a direction 'pointing' from a certain past, through the moment of action in the present, to a more or less uncertain future – with it being really possible at the present time for the world to be developed in any one of a number of different possible ways in the future by the actions of agents.

Some time ago, William James (1917: 150–1) compared *determinism* and *indeterminism* in terms precisely relevant to our concerns here, so I can do no better than to quote now what he had to say:

Determinism professes that those parts of the universe already laid down absolutely appoint and decree what the other parts shall be. The future has no ambiguous possibilities hidden in its womb: the part we call the present is compatible with only one totality. Any other future complement than the one fixed from eternity is impossible. The whole is in each and every part, and welds it with the rest into an absolute unity, an iron block, in which there can be no equivocation or shadow of turning.

Indeterminism, on the contrary, says that the parts have a certain amount of loose play on one another, so that the laying down of one of them does not necessarily determine what the others shall be. It admits that things not yet determined may really in themselves be ambiguous. Of two alternative futures which we conceive, both may now be really possible; and the one become impossible only at the moment when the other excludes it by becoming real itself. Indeterminism thus denies the world to be one unbending unit of fact. It says that there is a certain ultimate pluralism in it; and, so saying, it corroborates our ordinary unsophisticated view of things. To that view, actualities seem to float in a wider sea of possibilities from out of which they are chosen; and, *somewhere*, indeterminism says, such possibilities exist, and form a part of truth.

Action in an indeterministic world

Let us turn now to see what might happen in our new indeterministic world. Firstly, we must point out that, irrespective of whether we stop to deliberate before we act or not, any sort of action in an indeterministic world involves selection or choice. For, as James remarks, realizing one among a set of possibilities excludes the rest; to do anything in such a world is to do this and not that. And this is a point which creates difficulties for any thoroughgoing empiricist determined to couch all his accounts only in terms of what he can observe, in terms of the already realized world. In an indeterministic world, the meaning or significance of people's actions can only be assessed in the context of what they might have done but did not actually do – real possibilities do exist, and, as James says, do form a part of truth. This, however, is by the way here, where the main point I want to make is that action in an indeterministic world is in itself essentially selective. Or, as there is not always a clear field of possibilities from which selections are made, it might be better to say that it intrinsically leads to *determination*: action may make more determinate what is for us an indeterminate world.

Characterizing action in this way, as practical activity, as movement with a consequence, necessarily involves agents in the world, for the resistance of something other than themselves is necessary to the possibility of agents being able to act at all: to act is to act on something. Thus agents can only exist in processes of exchange with that which is 'other than' themselves; they are necessarily defined in relation to that which is 'outside' their agency. And what seems to be the case with people is that they can come to act with a knowledge or an awareness of the resistance that 'that which is other than themselves' will offer to their actions. In other words, they can come to act *intentionally*, not blindly, their actions informed by their knowledge of what they are acting on. However, this clearly cannot always be the case for them, especially in infancy. Lacking experience of their circumstances, they lack knowledge of what they can do and what they can be in relation to them. Thus people are not always in a position to deliberate, determine projects for themselves and then set out, intentionally, to achieve them. Often people, and especially infants, must distinguish themselves and their abilities from those of others in the course of ongoing exchanges. The person's own self and the selves of others are both then discovered together in relation to one another; they are reciprocally determined within the same categories as one another. In other words, to be me, I need you: I need you to respond to my movements for me to appreciate that my movements have consequences in you; I need you to respond to the meaning in my action for me to be able to appreciate that my action does in fact have a meaning. It is only in the course of

110

ongoing practical exchanges that meaning emerges, as Mead (1934) has maintained. And as I acquire, in the course of my exchanges with others, knowledge of their responses to my actions, I can come to act in the knowledge of those responses; I can come to act intending meanings in my action.

In the classical world it was man's task as a thinker to gain intellectual mastery over it, in the hope that this would lead in many cases to a technical mastery also (the power to rearrange what already exists). But in an indeterminate world, as may be expected, many of the sharp distinctions possible in theory are blunted in practice – mind and body, subject and object, self and other, even personality and personality, interpenetrate one another everywhere and continually – and it thus becomes man's task to make what is indeterminate determinate in whatever ways he can, according to his own needs and interests. In an indeterminate world man's central task becomes that of giving form to the act of living itself; it is up to him to imagine new possibilities for being human, new ways of how to live, and to attempt to realize them in practice – and this is essentially a moral (and a political) task, not just an intellectual one.

Time and the negotiation of social reality

It is as we pass from aspiration to achievement, from possibility to actuality, that we express ourselves: time is thus the essential psychological medium. And just as we have already lost the sharp distinctions between body and mind, and so on, so we also lose the sharp distinction between 'inner' mental activity and 'outer' bodily activity. Treating time realistically, not simply like a fourth dimension of space, but as the passage from possibility to actuality, suggests that our thoughts and feelings are not wholly private expressions, contained just within our bodies, but that we can (and usually do) show our thoughts and feelings, moods, beliefs, intentions, desires, etc., 'in' our bodily activity – it is only at a relatively late age that we learn to dissemble and keep our thoughts to ourselves. All that we express 'out there' in the world is informed one way

111

or another by our mentality; even 'doing nothing' may express a meaning.

However, categorizing such activity in order to make sense of it and account for it presents problems. For, as there is always more to come of processes in time, such activity is always intrinsically incomplete. It would seem that, in attempting to decide to which intersubjective categories such activities should be assigned, we should refer not only to spatial but to temporal criteria. Such temporal criteria, however, would be contingent; that is, they would be essentially incomplete, and determining them (making them 'as if' complete) one way or another is a matter of human choice. Thus if they are to be made 'logically adequate', to have the same kind of formal quality as spatial criteria, then *negotiation* with others as to the nature of their completed form is necessarily involved. Space prevents fuller discussion of this issue, but some discussion of it can be found in Harré and Secord (1972) and Shotter (1974a). Suffice it here to say this: to structure our perceptions of a person it would seem that we must specify a set of both spatial and temporal categories and place him in relation to them. In categorizing him spatially we can determine the nature of his objective structure and locate it, outside ourselves, in space. In categorizing him temporally we can determine his mental structure ... but where should we locate it? This is what has always puzzled us about mental activity: because there is nowhere precisely in space to locate it, neither in the observer nor the observed, it seems to float ethereally somewhere in between, and, lacking any substantiality, seems to have no real existence. In the classical world of matter in motion it has no place. But in an indeterministic world developing through real time it has its location in time. It can be located in people's shared history, and it is that which is amenable to specification. Thus it is via the structuring of our history that we can attempt to determine our future; but if we are concerned to act always responsibly, in a way that makes sense to others, then how we do structure it is not a matter entirely up to us alone – we must negotiate it with others.

The constraining, though not predetermining influence of

the past is an essential feature of development in an indeterministic, temporal world. Action thus does not come out of nowhere; it emerges from a definite past, through a particular present actuality, and may be directed towards one of a definite set of future possibilities. To turn away from determinism, and to allow a world in which there is a degree of loose jointedness, in which play can exist in every sense of the word (Shotter, 1973), is not then to turn to a miraculous world of disorderly events. It is simply to turn to a world with a real future, a future of limited but real alternatives which are made possible by what has been done in the past and by what is being done now.

Becoming

Our discussion of space and time has taken us into deep waters, but there is still a sense in which it is clearly inadequate. For, like all the other sharp distinctions in an indeterministic world, space and time also lose their independence from one another and to some extent merge – with time coming to take priority over space as the source of new possibilities. Instead of the world being thought of as simply being in space and changing through a spatialized time in which there are no passages from possibility to actuality, only rearrangements of what already exists, it is best thought of as an 'extensive becoming' (Čapek, 1965) in which relatively independent processes may develop alongside one another. But we can discuss this no further here; it is a theoretical problem for the future. The discussion above will suffice if it conveys some hints of the unique properties of time, and shows that we may have been quite mistaken to think of it merely as like a fourth dimension of space. Till recently in Western thought we have tried to reduce *becoming* to *being*, *process* to *substance*, *transformation* to *rearrangement*, *time* to *space*, *actions* to *events*, and *events* to *things*; we have attempted to give 'true reality' a static character, and, as one of the characters in Beckett's *Endgame* puts it, 'to put everything in its last place under its last dust'. But while the past has been determined (and determined by man in at least some degree), the future remains to be so. It is the future, not this or that hidden region of space, that holds rich promise of new possibilities.

By discussing agency, indeterminacy and time in this way, I have attempted to indicate that the fact that people are parts of a developing world is all of a piece with the fact that they grow up and can learn, realize intentions, express meanings, pursue projects, create novelties, play, and so on. In other words, I hope that by appreciating in broad outline how it is that we live through time, it will be possible to see that the mental activity which we called a 'fiction' in the past is truly real. And that psychology may be seen as the science which, by operating in an indeterministic world in which both logic and history can function in determining our future, can help us make clear to ourselves the possibilities open to us now from which we may choose our next step.

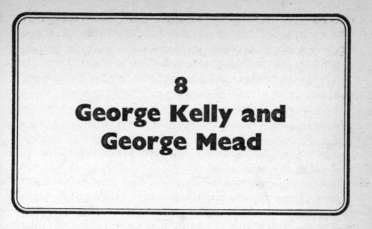

8
George Kelly and George Mead

If this could have been a somewhat longer book I would have turned to a fuller discussion, not so much of developing, organic structures themselves, but, bearing in mind Heisenberg's comments quoted earlier (Chapter 6, p. 88), a discussion of our knowledge of them. For, even though an organic form of order still fails to encompass our sense or ourselves as personal agencies, it manifests nonetheless many interesting and important properties not present in mechanical forms. And many things unintelligible when described in mechanical terms – such as, for instance, the nature of our knowledge – are rendered more comprehensible in organic terms. My purpose can be served, however, indirectly, by discussing what seem to me to be two important transitional figures in the development of a psychology of personal action: they each introduce important aspects of an image of ourselves as persons. Firstly, I shall discuss George Kelly's (1955) theory of *personal constructs* (see D3), in which he proposes an essentially organic form for the character of our knowledge. However, because as Neisser says, 'if we do not postulate some agent ... we must think of every thought and every response as just the momentary resultant of an interacting system', and because such a theory of our knowledge cannot encompass us, ourselves (only our *knowledge* of ourselves), I shall next discuss George

Mead's (1934) distinction between the 'I' and the 'me'. As aspects of the self, the 'me' is inconceivable without the 'I' (to conceive it), but the 'I' can only enter its own consciousness, Mead suggests, as a 'me', as an object of its own knowledge. There always remains, then, an indeterminate but active part of ourselves, available for further development.

George Kelly and the psychology of personal constructs

Kelly (1955) begins by pointing out that most psychological theories, those of man the machine or of man the biological organism, for instance, fail to account for the behaviour of those who devise and use such theories. He, himself, would have liked to have produced a theory of man the scientist, a truly *reflexive* theory in which his theory of man would have been of man with a theory. In this, however, he did not entirely succeed (Shotter, 1970b), for personal construct theory as such is more a theory of the structure of theories and how they are used than it is a theory of the nature of man *in toto* (Bannister and Fransella, 1971). This much said, let us turn now to an account of Kelly's theory.

The fundamental postulate in Kelly's (1955) theory is that 'a person's processes are psychologically channelized by the ways in which he anticipates events'. And Kelly thinks of people as being able to anticipate events by 'construing' the situations they are in by placing 'constructs' or 'construct systems' upon them – construing them in one way using one construct system and in another using another. Now my purpose here is not to show how close Kelly's notions are to those of rule and concept guided behaviour discussed by philosophers recently – Mischel (1964), for instance, does that – but to give an account of construct systems and to point out the organic aspect of their structure.

Unlike the attempt to characterize a concept by listing the features meant to be common to all the things to which the concept is applied, constructs are formed by considering not just things we think similar to one another, but also others which contrast with them. A construct may thus be thought of as a distinguishing or distinctive feature. And, in fact, the formation of a construct system is best thought of as being concerned with defining and distinguishing out the parts of some otherwise amorphous totality.

For example, in Fig. 8.1, think of f (flux) as some as yet, say, unanalysed speech noise: stage 1. After experiencing it for a while, we may begin to distinguish between periods of,

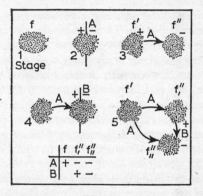

Fig. 8.1

say, relative variability $(A+)$ and relative constancy $(A-)$: stage 2. Having distinguished the two parts and set them over against one another, we must remember that they are still related to one another as parts of the same whole: stage 3. Within the more constant episodes $(A-)$ we may then notice, say, a relative presence $(B+)$ and a relative absence $(B-)$ of hiss: stage 4. And, again, after having noted the difference we must also remember the relation: stage 5. And so on: the totality of the flux may be differentiated further, or in relation to quite different features, as exigencies demand; constructs have, as Kelly says, 'a range of convenience'.

The process serves to structure a whole into a set of inter-

117

related parts, the character of each part being known in terms of its relations to all the others in the system – they are all still parts of f, but now they are 'characterized' parts. Unlike the attempt to characterize things in isolation from one another by abstracting common features, the parts here are reciprocally determined, all in relation to one another. Each has its significance in the context provided by the rest; one unit cannot be changed without changing the character of the whole. And, while perceptually distinguishable, the parts cannot be physically isolated from one another without destroying the set of relations constituting the whole.

Construing or differentiating a totality into a system of interrelated parts by use of a construct system does two things: (1) it identifies each part just as much in terms of features it does not have in common with others as those it does – things are known both in terms of what they are and what they are not; and (2) parts are defined not by what they are in themselves but by the part they play in relation to all the other parts constituting the whole. Thus we have here then the kind of system discussed by Dewey as an organic structure, in which the parts are known in terms of their *value* or *function*, by what they are doing in the system rather than by any formal qualities they may have when considered in isolation from one another. Such a form of order as this is of quite a different kind to mechanical forms of order, consisting of objective parts.

Our knowledge of our knowledge

In discussing Kelly's personal construct theory, we have been dealing with a system for *characterizing* the structure of our knowledge. But we must remember that to characterize a form of knowledge is not to render that knowledge itself explicit. In other words, we have been dealing here, as we remarked at the outset, not with organic forms of order directly, but with our knowledge of them, i.e. with, in Kelly's case, the

118

character of our knowledge of our knowledge, for his is a theory of theories. The reflexive, self-referential nature of our endeavour here is plain. And that is the point: while we may construct new constructions or elaborate old ones, we can never escape from within their confines to a direct, self-conscious grasp of things in themselves. As embodied beings we may, as Dreyfus points out, directly *sense* them in a vague and global manner. But unless we can internally articulate and structure our vague sense of our situation and place it in relation to a meaningful scheme of things, we cannot decide in particular how to take it and modify it to our requirements – the thing men can do which animals, in general, cannot. However, determining the character of a thing in order to deal with it brings us back once again within the realm of our constructions and interpretations – within what some call the 'hermeneutical circle' (Taylor, 1971). While we may expand that circle, every problem we meet originates within it, and every solution we find must return to it. Our self-conscious grasp of things is, as Neisser claims, an intrinsically mediated affair, an affair mediated by our own constructions and our own interpretations.

George Mead's theory of the self

Remembering the distinction made earlier between 'tools' and 'objects', we may say about our selves that we both have a body and are a body: while clearly being unable to exist without a body, it is as if we can 'use' our bodies on occasions at least in the execution of our intentions.

Now the first thing that Mead (1934: 139) does in his discussion of the self is to distinguish between the self and the body:

The self has a character which is different from that of the physiological organism proper. The self is something which has a development; it is not initially there at birth, but arises in the process of social experience and activity....

119

In the light of our discussion above, it may be best to add that it is not so much that the human organism is necessarily born without a sense of its own functioning, but clearly it is necessarily born without any knowledge of the character of its sense of its own functioning. It is not so much the self that arises, then, in the process of social experience, as the articulated character of the self. Isolated from social exchanges, we can only presume that the self would remain vague and indeterminate. This much said in criticism, let us now return to Mead's account.

For Mead, then, the self (we would say its character) is a social structure, whereas, of course, the body as an organic, structuring structure is not. And whereas the self can know itself as an object, the body cannot. The body as an organism can act only as it must according to its own devices – 'the self is not necessarily involved in the life of the organism', says Mead (1934: 136). But the self does become involved in those situations where one responds to one's own activity as others respond to it; the self is involved in the socially meaningful acts of the organism. And the aspect of the self which becomes known to itself as an object in all of this, which Mead terms the 'me', becomes known in terms of the responses of others to my actions.

This is just to repeat what we have said before. However, after discussing the social origins of the self, Mead then asks what is the nature of the 'I' which is aware of the social 'me'? We can only assume that the 'I' (like the Freudian 'id') is rooted in bodily activity and as such cannot know itself as an object. But, he says, the 'I' reacts to the self which arises through the taking of the attitudes of others. Through taking those attitudes we have introduced the 'me' and we react to it as an 'I' (1934: 174). Thus we can have, so to speak, conversations with ourselves, through our different 'mes'. The 'I' is the unique, active, idiosyncratic, subjective and essentially indeterminate aspect of an individual personality, the source of our sense of freedom, initiative, and puzzlement as to the extent of ourselves: the 'me' is the passive, objective, empirical, relatively stable aspect of ourselves existing for others. Here as elsewhere in living processes, it must be presumed that there is a continual dialectic, a continual back and forth of distinguishable but inseparable processes reciprocally determining one another's character. The 'I', though, is clearly the 'leading' part, for as Mead (1934:178) says, 'the "I" calls out the "me" and responds to it'.

While the 'I' must remain, then, as forever outside the circle of our characterizations, it is necessary to presuppose its existence as the condition of our being able to have, acquire and use any knowledge at all. Thus, even now, we may say that we do not know fully what we are or what we might become. The exciting prospect of discovering how to be more than we already are lies before us. To others, though, such as Neisser, who are concerned with the classical scientific task of discovering the one true image of man for all time, such a creative dialectic appears as an unfortunate infinite regress. And they hope to escape from it:

> It now seems possible that there is an escape from the regress that formerly seemed infinite. As recently as a generation ago, processes of control had to be thought of as *homunculi*, because man was the only known model of an executive agent. Today, the stored-program computer has provided us with an alternative possibility, in the form of the *executive routine*. This is a concept which may be of considerable use to psychology. (1967:295)

But if the approach here is correct Neisser's hope is forlorn: while the self may know itself as an object, the 'I' cannot. There is always more to come of processes developing in time – 'I' am not finished yet.

From Kelly and Mead to a personal form of order

Let us return to our fundamental anchor point for a psychology of personal action, and try to outline its form to contrast it with Kelly's and Mead's psychology: rather than contemplation, we have taken action – what we do – as providing us with our primary access to reality. And we have suggested that it is only through taking action that we acquire knowledge of both what is 'inside' and 'outside' us; the one being reciprocally determined in relation to the other. But we have gone further than this: a man acts in relation to other men, he is a person in a community of persons. In fact, we have suggested that it is only in the personal relation of persons that personal existence comes into being – that persons cannot come into existence in isolation but only through communication with one another. Their *persona* as individual personalities, the knowledge of the 'positions' that they may assume in their community, their knowledge of their *selves*, is something they acquire after birth, in the course of communicative exchanges with their fellows. But if it is the communications a man receives after birth that are crucial in determining his personal existence, it means that men are not like organisms, who have their species-specific nature communicated to them before birth, genetically rather than culturally. It means, in other words, that men are not organisms, and that the personal form of order must be distinguished from the organic (just as the organic must be distinguished from the mechanical). And in it the social, cultural and historical must be distinguished from the natural, biological and evolutionary, for it is in these spheres that personally important events occur.

In our psychology of personal action, practical activity has been taken to be primary; theoretical activity, if it occurs at all, emerges from it and serves to modify it. In action, knowledge and movement are integrated: action is movement informed by knowledge. In the classical Cartesian scheme of things, movement and knowledge are considered as existing in isolation from one another. Descartes begins with the *Cogito*, with the fact that 'I think' is indubitable. And setting himself over against the world, he merely observes that motions happen within it. Thus classically, theoretical activity, thinking, is taken to be primary, and there is a bewildering puzzle as to how the motions man can observe and describe as taking place in the world can ever become informed or otherwise influenced by his knowledge. Furthermore, attending only to what he can observe 'outside' himself and ignoring what he can sense 'within' himself, he values only the knowledge he acquires of objects and neglects the knowledge he acquires of how to act. Thus failing to distinguish these two forms of knowledge – the knowledge we have of things and the knowledge we have of how to use them – he thinks of his knowledge of things as being the only kind of knowledge there can be. But such knowledge does not inform action.

Both Kelly and Mead may with justice be said not to have fully worked through to the revolutionary conclusions implicit in some of their own proposals. Considering the reflexive nature of their endeavours – the fact that they were seeking to understand how, among other things, we understand ourselves – they should, ideally, have presented their theories within a framework of thought that was derived from their own theories! Instead we must assess them as transitional figures, for while they present much that is new, they retain something of the old views too. But would we not be asking for the impossible, to ask for a total change in one step? For, as mentioned earlier, if what we do is to be meaningful, it must be related in some clear way to what has already been done. Thus while a whole may be changed eventually in every respect, if it is to be qualitatively transformed, only a part at a time may be changed. Both Kelly and Mead retain the classical emphasis upon objective knowledge and fail to consider use-knowledge. They attempt to develop a psychology of action, not from a standpoint in action but from one in thought, as observers of men's activities. Nonetheless, the images of man they attempted to produce, the image of man the scientist (Kelly), and man with a social self (Mead), are transitional images of crucial importance in our attempts to escape from our image of ourselves as a chance amalgam of matter in blind but lawful motion.

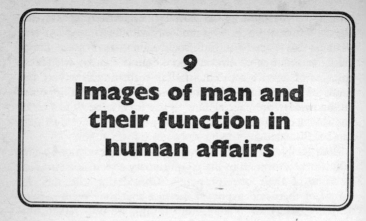

9
Images of man and their function in human affairs

I have discussed, then, three different patterns of arrangement, three forms of order: the mechanical, the organic and the personal. The formal structure of the mechanical can be made as explicit as one could wish, and mathematical theories of it abound (Arbib, 1964; Minsky, 1967). Such theories describe the behaviour of things independently of any responsibility that we might have for what they do. Once we turn, however, to organisms and to people, entities who only exist in a state of exchange with their circumstances, the responsibility we may or may not have for what they do is more difficult to assess. We must take into account our relations to such entities in our attempts to determine their nature. Thus it is not surprising to find that the formal structure of the organic is still somewhat problematical and a matter for current research (Bertalanffy, 1968; Piaget, 1971), while the form of the personal is even more obscure. What is clear, though, is that organisms cannot be reduced to mechanisms (though organisms may contain mechanisms), and people cannot be reduced to either organisms or mechanisms (though they may contain both).

In discussing these three forms of order I have, following Macmurray (1957, 1961), suggested that instead of taking the classical standpoint of the egocentric, outside observer, we adopt the standpoint of the socially responsible person, immersed in the world in a community with other persons; that we take the 'I-and-you do' standpoint rather than the 'I think'. In this book, however, more than just those two standpoints have been discussed, so let me abstract from my discussion a schema which may help to place a little more order on my earlier commentaries:

<pre>
                              standpoints
                           ⏞
                           I   I-and-you
                 ⎧Mechanical
Forms of order ⎨Organic
                 ⎩Personal
                              think   do
</pre>

The schema defines four possible standpoints, and thus twelve possible approaches. But only one approach, that studying people from a standpoint in the 'I-and-you do' within a personal form of order, is reflexive in the sense that standpoint and form of order are mutually inclusive. Furthermore, of the approaches I have discussed, not all are pure forms in relation to this idealized scheme; some are rather mixed. It is for this reason that I did not commit myself at the outset to such a Procrustean bed of categories as this; practice, at least for me, has preceded theory in this respect. However, while many may disagree with my assignments, there may be some value now in placing those I have mentioned in the categories provided by such a schema.

(1) Weiskrantz clearly attempts to study man as a machine from the standpoint of an external observer, the 'I think' standpoint. This is the classical approach. (2) Dewey complains that old mechanical conceptions are still in control, so he gives an organic account of human activity, adopting a mixed but egocentric standpoint, referring sometimes to observational and sometimes to experiential criteria – the 'I think' and the 'I do' standpoints. (3) Neisser also adopts a mixed approach. He studies man as a machine from the classical standpoint, but a machine controlled by an executive

agent. (4) Dreyfus, however, takes his standpoint in action, in the 'I do'. Lacking any account of creative social exchanges constitutive of personal existence, of dialogue, he ends simply by giving an account of man as an organism, an 'embodied agent'. (5) Kelly's approach is difficult to characterize, for his works are littered with illuminating comments from many points of view. However, he seems to focus on man as an executive agent who uses organic structures (construct systems) in order to anticipate events. And in investigating construct systems by the repertory grid technique (see Bannister and Fransella, 1971), centres himself in the classical standpoint. (6) Mead too is bewildering. He attempts to treat persons as organisms with emergent selves, aware of other selves. And he appears to adopt a standpoint in the 'I-and-you think'. Thus while he may have much to say about our knowledge of who or what we *are*, how we ever come to *do* things still puzzles us. (7) Finally, the approach that I have attempted to introduce here is (nearly) Macmurray's, in which man is studied from a standpoint in the 'I-and-you do', within the form of the personal.

These are some, just some of the images of man which have been and which might be used to inform and structure research in psychology. But not only psychology, in daily life too. Whenever we alone are trying to decide for ourselves what we are going to do next, we can only refer to our image of ourselves for knowledge of who and what we are and what we can try to become. Such an image of our own nature must be one of our most priceless possessions, for without it we would be unable to deliberate upon or plan our own future – to take up our circumstances and bend them as we require rather than being bent by them as they require. Thus such images influence how we live. And there is ample scope for debate about that, debate which can be informed by the logical structure of the alternative concepts of ourselves we elucidate, not by the emotional polemics the experimentalists fear if every statement is not an induction from laboratory data.

And debate there must and will be. In such a debate, I would suggest that since the characterization of our nature was a conceptual rather than an empirical matter, it is not a matter of 'waiting to see' what empirical research will show to be the case, but a matter of elucidating the implications in the concepts of ourselves that we do in fact use in our everyday practices (empirical research would, as outlined in Chapter 2, then be concerned with exploring the further realization of such possibilities inherent in our concepts). This is what I mean when I propose that psychology should become a *moral* or a *hermeneutical* science of man: that it should be a science concerned not with objective things 'outside' our agency to control, but with our interpretations and meanings, our concepts and their interpretations – with specifying the possibilities open to us in theory that we might choose to try to realize them in practice. 'But we cannot hide from ourselves', says Taylor (1971:51):

> how greatly this option breaks with certain commonly held notions about our scientific traditions. We cannot measure such sciences (moral or hermeneutical ones) against the requirements of a science of verification: we cannot judge them by their predictive capacity. We have to accept that they are founded on intuitions which all do not share, and what is worse that these intuitions are closely bound up with our fundamental options (about how to live). These sciences cannot be 'wertfrei' [value free]; they are moral sciences in a more radical sense than the eighteenth century understood. Finally, their successful prosecution requires a high degree of freedom from illusion, in the sense of error which is rooted and expressed in one's way of life; for our incapacity to understand is rooted in our own self-definitions, hence in what we are. To say this is not to say anything new: Aristotle makes a similar point in Book 1 of the *Ethics*. But it is still radically shocking and unassimilable to the mainstream of modern science.

We have, I feel, no choice in psychology but to assimilate it. The alternative is the total fragmentation of psychology into an aggregate of specialisms lacking all coherence. However, by conducting a reflexive psychology from a standpoint in action, rather than by trying to observe behaviour from the outside, this fragmentation can be avoided: all the different theories of nature and of human nature that people produce can be seen as emerging from, and returning to modify, different forms of human action – action for which the reasons can be found. A standpoint in action can thus transcend all specialist views, and provide a standpoint for the understanding of all that people do.

10
The human nature
of human nature

While one may refer to Darwin and claim to be taking an evolutionary rather than a static, mechanical view of man, it is still not enough. One must not ignore the importance of the fact that for man, unlike any other animals, life is a task. Unlike any other beings, our actual mode of existence, our form of living is not given to us ready made along with our material form: we have to make it up, in its detailed, moment to moment form, for ourselves. It is this more than anything else that makes the form of the organic inadequate for the understanding of people's actions: people must deliberate upon what they are going to try to do next in order to maintain themselves, and all the paraphernalia of rationality comes into play in such deliberations. It is thus that we must introduce a new and distinct order of categories, richer but inclusive of organic forms, for the description of such action: the form of the personal.

Nature and culture

Certainly life in general is given to us: we do not give it to ourselves. But suddenly we seem to find ourselves in the midst of it without quite knowing how we came to exist and what is involved in continuing to exist. We must live, but how?

There is very little that we just find ourselves doing, without it having been thought about and planned, no matter how dimly, if not by ourselves then by others, now or at some time in the past. As far as we can tell, we are under no compulsion to do anything in particular at all. Of course we must eat: but what? Of course we must drink: but what? Of course we all experience sexual sensations: but how exactly should they be acted upon? Unlike the trees and the stars, the birds and the bees, we do not have a species-specific way of going on; it is up to us to maintain ourselves in existence as best we can. We have to be agents in the process of our own survival; it does not happen automatically. In the past, man has interpreted his necessity to face this task as due to his 'fall': noting that all else seemed to rest unconcerned in the cradle of nature, he felt that it was because he ate from the 'tree of knowledge' that he was cast out of the 'Garden of Eden' and, made aware of right and wrong, forced to fend for himself.

But nowhere is man to be found in a state of nature. Everywhere and at every time he is only to be found in a state of culture, living ways of life that he must have devised for himself in some way – ways of life that his young inherit, not genetically like blue eyes, but in a process of communication which takes place after birth. It is this, as Chein (1972) suggests, that is his defining characteristic, i.e. he is self-defining.

However, we shall not treat his separation from the rest of creation as a fall but as an ascent – an achievement to be marvelled at rather than a crime demanding atonement. However, whether ascent or descent, psychologists who ignore the fact that men experience life as a task ignore also the fact that men, in the execution of that task, have transformed themselves from what they once were in history to what they are now. Man has invented for himself, besides the more tangible and material things of his present-day world, forms of critical thought, mathematics and calculation, forms of theorizing, forms of imaginative expression and rational investigation (in the attempt to correct many of his mistaken inventions!); he has invented many forms of social institution, among them

130

even the natural sciences (and he attempts now to construct human sciences!); in short, man has made himself. And the process continues.

Some of the artefacts and skills, the human products and processes we have mentioned, were the results of deliberate invention by men whose names are known and remembered; deservedly so, for they brought into existence aspects of our humanity which did not previously exist. Often, though, important inventions have happened spontaneously, as if by accident, and the real heroes who made us men so long ago go unsung: they could not make history until they had invented what made the recording of history possible. And what an important invention that was, for only men who possess a history are able to compare what they are now with what they once were, and judge whether there is any improvement or not. Thus, 'human history is not', Winch (1958:64) remarks, 'just an account of changing habits: it is the study of how men tried to carry over what they regard as important in their modes of behaviour into the new situations which they have had to face'. And people who know no history, so the aphorism runs, are condemned to repeat its mistakes – this is presumably the fate too of a psychology which respects its own history insufficiently.

Human history, then, is a record of how men have changed as a result of their own efforts and the choices that they have made. It is not a record of how they have evolved naturally. 'We are not organisms but persons', remarks Macmurray (1961:46),

The nexus of relations which unite us in a human society is not organic but personal. Human behaviour cannot be understood, but only caricatured, if it is represented as an adaptation to an environment; and there is no such process as social evolution but, instead, a history which reveals a precarious development and possibilities of both progress and retrogression.

The slow but continued improvement of ourselves is not a necessary process, guaranteed to our species; our humanity may be lost at any time.

It is not nature but we ourselves who are responsible for making and maintaining ourselves as distinct from the beasts and all else that there is. We can, so to speak, intend the distinction, and it is up to us to determine it how we can and how we will. Thus we call that by which we distinguish ourselves, our humanity; it is that which we possess and which organisms and machines do not. But the fact that it is *we* who make the characteristics which distinguish us from all else that there is makes us qualitatively distinct from the rest of creation: *man is a self-defining animal*, as we have said before.

But, to repeat, it is a human task to intend and to maintain such distinctions. And it is interesting to see how many activities in human life, while ostensibly serving other purposes, are directed to maintaining the boundary between ourselves and the rest of nature: while cleaning may be necessary for hygiene, cleanliness *is* next to godliness, for it marks the distinction between purity and impurity (Douglas, 1966). Dirt must be removed from sacred places as it is 'out of place', untidy, unruly; it flouts the purity of the form of order by which we live our lives in that sphere. It might endanger our activities there, if for no other than the mundane reason that it distracts our attention from the details of what we do in that situation.

It is also interesting to see how great revolutions in thought have borne upon this distinction – perhaps because man has so often interpreted his task in life as that of regaining a lost paradise. Whether this is the case or not, recent concern with this boundary has mostly been to do with its destruction. As mentioned in Chapter 1, Darwin's proposals are mostly interpreted as indicating not that men are distinct from the apes but the opposite; men are seen as descended rather than ascended from them. Freud's discovery of the 'unconscious' and the 'id' has tended to emphasize the animal in man, as has modern ethology (Lorenz, 1966), and so called naked apery (Morris, 1967). And no sooner had Descartes drawn a distinction between mind and matter, than Hobbes began the line of thought which continues into the present day determined to abolish it. So the conflict between nature and culture is real, and as Broadbent (1961:11) comments, 'While ... most modern thought has continued to divide human beings sharply from the natural phenomena around them, an attack upon this division has been quietly growing in strength.' It has grown to such an extent that many (Cassirer, 1944; Matson, 1964, for instance) would say that man now faces a crisis in his knowledge of himself: he has forgotten that he makes himself and is hoping mistakenly to find the principles for his own improvement in nature – Broadbent is too modest: the attack is not quietly growing, it is all but complete. The results, however, have been most unfortunate.

As natural scientists, psychologists have attached little importance to the fact that man's first need is the need to become a person (and that, throughout his life, it perhaps remains his deepest need). They have searched for the laws of behaviour applicable to any human beings whatsoever (just as Newton's laws may be applied to any point masses whatsoever). And such general laws, with features common, presumably, to cave men, wild boys, aboriginals, modern Western men, etc., exclude at the outset what we, at this moment, call our humanity. As a natural science psychology has no place for our humanity in it at all. As a moral scientist, the psychologist appreciates that while nature may provide the materials for man's human nature, it is man himself who must make it. And it is the psychologist's job here to understand how it is done, studying how it happens spontaneously in order later to be able to do it deliberately. This is the task of psychology as a moral science of action rather than a natural science of behaviour.

Becoming what we believe ourselves to be

Man must give form to his act of living. This is just as true for an individual as it is for a group of people living in a community. Each individual, if he is to be self-determining and not continually acting in a mistaken fashion, must reflect time and again before he acts; determine theoretically what he is going to try to do before trying to do it in practice. But such reflection and deliberation is impossible unless one possesses certain prior beliefs: beliefs about the world, other men, and oneself. Only in the light of such convictions is it possible to determine a preference in theory for one line of action over another. Men's lives depend, then, fundamentally upon the beliefs in which their self-conscious acts are grounded. And it follows from this that the most decisive changes in the nature of our humanity are changes in our beliefs about ourselves.

It matters, then, what we believe ourselves to be: particularly, it matters whether we believe our actions to be 'caused' – directly by our environment and indirectly by our genes (Skinner) – or whether we believe that we ourselves can determine what we do. Quite different practical consequences, quite different social policies, flow from grounding our actions in one of these beliefs rather than the other.

While many psychologists are exploring the consequences of grounding our actions in beliefs appropriate to the conduct of a natural science, in this book we have begun to explore the possibility of grounding our actions in a belief in ourselves: a belief that we can determine in one way or another what we do. And the most important task we now face, I feel, is that of determining what we are going to do with ourselves in the future. But until we possess the belief that man can be more fully human, and regain our nerve, our confidence in ourselves, the task cannot even be begun. This book is part of the attempt to make that belief at least seem a reasonable one – at least as reasonable, that is, as the belief that we are nothing but a collection of atoms and molecules in senseless movement.

However, although we may distinguish ourselves from all else that there is, we must remember that we remain nonetheless a part of it all. While we may 'intend' the distinction and live our lives upon its basis, we can never physically separate ourselves from the rest of creation. The nature of man is thus intrinsically and eternally problematic: we must make and continually remake our own nature, we must constantly be in search of ourselves. But we cannot discover the nature of ourselves in the same way that we can discover the nature of things 'outside' us. Physical things may be described in terms of their objective properties, but we may only be described in terms of the beliefs by which we live – the character of our consciousness. And this is not to be discovered as an empirical thing. It is only in our immediate exchanges with others that we express and reveal our selves to them, and they their selves to us. The truth about people, about human nature, then, is not something that is awaiting discovery, ready made, like something under a stone on the beach: it can only be made by people in dialogue, as the product of a social act, in continual mutual interrogation and reply.

The new psychology of action we propose requires, thus, not just a change of content compared with the old, but a radical new form of thought and mode of investigatory activity. It aims at producing not publicly shared objective knowledge, but intersubjectively shared understandings, not discovered by individuals searching in the world alone, but made and agreed upon by people working in dialogue together.

Freedom and dignity

If the living of our lives were not a task, if our form of life were given us in our biology, if we were not free agents, then we should not find the problem of what we are so crucial. We would simply live as we must, as the appropriate biological directives within us decreed. However, experientially at least, *determinism* is not true: 'we are condemned to be free', says Sartre; we live lives full of uncertainty, and our freedom is a burden to us. We have to form our own principles, to shape our own conduct as agents in an intrinsically indeterminate world. And viewing ourselves like this puts the old free will versus determinism controversy in quite a new light: only men who are free agents are free to determine their own behaviour according to rigorous, logical and precise principles. It is not the man caused to move this way and that at the caprice of circumstances who shows order and principle in his conduct, but the man who keeps a principle firmly in mind and refuses to be distracted by circumstances. It is our freedom that makes the order in our lives possible.

Men who have lost their grasp on their ability to construct such principles for themselves, and hope to discover alternatives 'ready made' in nature, run the risk of losing their humanity and making themselves like all else in nature: into things caused to move by events 'outside' themselves.

The point that I want finally to recapitulate is this: man is not just man in nature, he is man in a culture in nature. And a man's culture is not to be characterized in terms of objective properties like all the other things that he sees in nature from within his culture. The culture from within which a man views the world and deliberates upon how to act in it structures his consciousness, and can only be characterized in terms of his beliefs (to be revealed by conceptual analyses, and all the other methods discussed earlier). Thus, if there is a key to the contemporary phase in the development of the human sciences, it is this: there is a third term to the relation between man and nature, *culture*, which is not genetically inherited but communicated to man after birth as a 'second nature'. It is this third term that psychology, in its attempts to be 'scientific', has ignored.

In the past men have invented many forms of expression for themselves, forms of language, writing, mathematics, painting, drama, forms of war and forms of peace, forms of family and community organization; in short, he has invented for himself his own forms of life. And there is no reason to suppose that the process by which we transformed ourselves from cave dwellers in the past to what we are now is at an end. Cultural progress is surely still possible, and a science called *psychology* can surely assist in making the future transformations of man more human ones, so that we can all in the future enhance one another's humanity. In the task ahead, the dignity, the self-respect, the confidence to believe that by acting freely we can become more fully human is essential. Beyond freedom and dignity (Skinner, 1972) is the human termite colony – if, indeed, man's nature could truly cease to be a self-determining one, as Skinner's vision would demand.

136

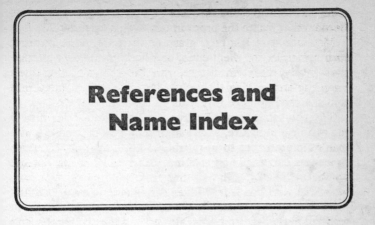

References and Name Index

The numbers in italics following each entry refer to page numbers within this book.

Arbib, M. (1964) *Brains, Machines and Mathematics.* New York: McGraw-Hill. *124*

Bannister, D. and Fransella (1971) *Inquiring Man.* Harmondsworth: Penguin. *116, 126*

Bartlett, F. (1932) *Remembering.* Cambridge: Cambridge University Press. *57*

Berger, P. L. and Luckman, T. (1967) *The Social Construction of Reality.* Harmondsworth: Penguin. *103*

Bernstein, B. (1972) *Class, Codes and Control.* London: Routledge and Kegan Paul. *98*

Bernstein, R. (1972) *Praxis and Action.* London: Duckworth. *85*

Bertalanffy, L. V. (1973) *General System Theory.* Harmondsworth: Penguin. *124*

Bower, T. G. R. (1966) The visual world of infants. *Scientific American,* 215: 80–92. Offprint no. 502. *19*

Bower, T. G. R. (1974) *Development in Infancy.* San Francisco: Freeman. *19*

Brand, C. (1971) Hercules's nervous breakdown? An appeal to psychology's pessimists. *Bull. Br. Psychol. Soc.* 24: 307–15. *73*

Broadbent, D. E. (1958) *Perception and Communication.* London: Pergamon. *26, 50*

Broadbent, D. E. (1961) *Behaviour*. London: Eyre and Spottis-woode. *133*

Broadbent, D. E. (1969) On distinguishing perception from memory. *Theoria to Theory 3*: 30–41. *42*

Broadbent, D. E. (1971) Cognitive psychology: introduction. *British Medical Bulletin 27* (3): 191–4. *52*

Broadbent, D. E. (1973) *In Defence of Empirical Psychology*. London: Methuen. *22*

Bronowski, J. (1973) *The Ascent of Man*. London: BBC. *9*

Campbell, F. W., Cooper, G. F. and Enroth-Cugell, C. (1969) The spatial selectivity of the visual cells of the cat. *J. Physiol. 203*: 223–35. *47*

Čapek, M. (1965) *The Philosophical Impact of Contemporary Physics*. New York: Van Nostrand. *113*

Cassirer, E. (1944) *Essay on Man*. Yale: Yale University Press. *133*

Chein, I. (1972) *The Image of Man and the Science of Behaviour*. London: Tavistock. *90, 91, 130*

Chomsky, N. (1965) *Aspects of the Theory of Syntax*. Cambridge, Mass.: M.I.T. *21, 97*

Dawson, R. W. K. (1974) Craik's premise: men and machines can be specified in the same terms. *Bull. Br. Psychol. Soc. 27*: 258–62. *72*

Dewey, J. (1896) The concept of the reflex arc in psychology. *Psychological Review 3*: 13–32. Reprinted in W. Dennis (ed.) *Readings in the History of Psychology*. New York: Appleton-Century-Crofts (1948). *50, 51, 54, 55, 118, 125*

Douglas, M. (1966) *Purity and Danger*. Harmondsworth: Penguin. *132*

Dreyfus, H. L. (1967) Why computers must have bodies in order to be intelligent. *Rev. Metaphysics 21*: 13–32. *62, 63, 64, 65, 66, 67, 126*

Eysenck, H. (1969) The technology of consent. *New Scientist 42* (655) (26 June): 688–90. *22*

Fantz, R. L. (1961) The origin of form perception. *Scientific American 204*: 66–72. Offprint no. 459. *19*

Gombrich, E. H. (1960) *Art and Illusion* (2nd ed.) London: Phaidon. *49*

Gregory, R. L. (1970) *The Intelligent Eye*. London: Weidenfeld and Nicolson. *49*

Gross, G. (1974) Unnatural selection. In N. Armistead (ed.) *Re-*

constructing Social Psychology. Harmondsworth: Penguin. *71*

Hampshire, S. (1959) *Thought and Action*. London: Chatto and Windus. *85*

Harré, R. (1970) Powers. *Brit. J. Philos. Sci. 21*: 81–101. *107*

Harré, R. (1971) Joynson's dilemma. *Bull. Br. Psychol. Soc. 24*: 115–19. *45, 46*

Harré, R. and Secord, P. F. (1972) *The Explanation of Social Behaviour*. Oxford: Blackwell. *112*

Heisenberg, W. (1958) *The Physicists' Conception of Nature*. London: Hutchinson. *88, 115*

Hubel, D. H. and Wiesel, T. N. (1962) Receptive fields, binocular interaction and functional architecture in the cat's visual cortex. *J. Physiol. 160*: 106–54. *47, 48*

Hull, C. L. (1943) *Principles of Behaviour*. New York: Appleton-Century-Crofts. *43, 81*

James. W. (1890) *Principles of Psychology*. London: Macmillan. *53, 106*

James, W. (1917) The dilemma of determinism. In *The Will to Believe and Other Essays in Popular Philosophy*. London: Longmans. *108*

Joynson, R. B. (1970) The breakdown of modern psychology. *Bull. Br. Psychol. Soc. 23*: 261–9. *45*

Joynson, R. L. (1972) The return of mind. *Bull. Br. Psychol. Soc. 25*: 1–10. *45, 46*

Kelly, G. (1955) *The Psychology of Personal Constructs* (2 vols). New York: Norton. *115, 116, 126*

Koch, S. (1964) Psychology and emerging conceptions of knowledge as unitary. In T. W. Wann (ed.) *Behaviourism and Phenomenology*. Chicago: University of Chicago Press. *16, 69*

Kuhn, T. S. (1962) *The Structure of Scientific Revolutions*. Chicago: Chicago University Press. *39*

Lashley, K. S. (1951) The problem of serial order in behaviour. In L. A. Jeffress (ed.) *Cerebral Mechanisms in Behavior*. New York: Wiley. *63*

Liberman, A. M., Cooper, F. S., Shankweiler, D. P. and Studdert-Kennedy, M. (1967) Perception of the speech code. *Psychol. Rev. 74*: 431–61. *97*

Lorenz, K. (1966) *On Aggression*. London: Methuen. *132*

McDougall, W. (1923) *Outline of Psychology*. London: Methuen. *43*

Macmurray, J. (1957) *The Self as Agent*. London: Faber and Faber. *23, 85, 124, 126*

Macmurray, J. (1961) *Persons in Relation*. London: Faber and Faber. *20, 23, 86, 124, 126, 131*

Magee, B. (1973) *Popper*. London: Fontana. *104*

Matson, F. W. (1964) *The Broken Image*. New York: Braziller. *133*

Mead, G. H. (1934) *Mind, Self and Society*. Chicago: University of Chicago Press. *20, 92, 93, 116, 120, 121, 126*

Mettler, F. (1955) Culture and the structural evolution of the neural system. In M. F. Ashley Montague (ed.) *Culture and the Evolution of Man*. New York: Oxford. *13*

Miller, G. A. (1969) Psychology as a means of promoting human welfare. *American Psychologist 24*: 1063–75. *25, 28, 29, 31, 33, 34, 82, 83*

Minsky, M. (1967) *Computation*. New York: Prentice-Hall. *124*

Mirandola, Pico della (1965) *The Dignity of Man* (trans. Wallis). New York: Bobbs-Merrill. *12*

Mischel, T. (1964) Personal constructs, rules, and the logic of clinical activity. *Psychological Review 71*: 180–92. *116*

Mischel, T. (ed.) (1969) *Human Action*. New York: Academic Press. *86*

Morris, D. (1967) *The Naked Ape*. London: Jonathan Cape. *132*

Neisser, U. (1967) *Cognitive Psychology*. New York: Appleton-Century-Crofts. *56, 57, 58, 61, 121, 125*

Newell, A., Shaw, J. C. and Simon, H. A. (1959) Report on a general problem-solving program. In D. Luce (ed.) *Readings in Mathematical Psychology*. New York: Wiley. *63*

Newson, J. and Shotter, J. (8 Aug. 1974) How babies communicate. *New Society 29* (618): 345–7. *99*

O'Neill, J. (1974) *Phenomenology, Language and Sociology: Selected Essays of Maurice Merleau-Ponty*. London: Heinemann. *41*

Peters, R. S. (1958) *The Conception of Motivation*. London: Routledge and Kegan Paul. *86*

Piaget, J. (1971) *Structuralism*. London: Routledge and Kegan Paul. *124*

Polanyi, M. (1958) *Personal Knowledge*. London: Routledge and Kegan Paul. *65*

Ryan, J. (1974) Early language development. In M. P. M.

Richards (ed.) *The Integration of a Child into a Social World*. Cambridge: Cambridge University Press. *99*

Ryle, G. (1949) *The Concept of Mind*. London: Hutchinson. *98*

Schaffer, H. R. (4 April, 1974) Behavioural synchrony in infancy. *New Scientist*. *99*

Schrodinger, E. (1967) *What is Life?* and *Mind and Matter*. Cambridge: Cambridge University Press (1st ed. 1943). *88*

Scriven, M. (1964) Views of human nature. In T. W. Wann (ed.) *Behaviourism and Phenomenology*. Chicago: University of Chicago Press. *46*

Sedgwick, P. (1974) Ideology in modern psychology. In N. Armistead (ed.) *Reconstructing Social Psychology*. Harmondsworth: Penguin. *69*

Sherrington, C. (1947) *The Integrative Action of the Nervous System*. Cambridge: Cambridge University Press. *46*

Shotter, J. (1970a) The philosophy of psychology: the psychological foundations of psychology. *Bull. Br. Psychol. Soc. 23*: 207–12. *69*

Shotter, J. (1970b) Men, the man-makers: George Kelly and the psychology of personal constructs. In D. Bannister (ed.) *Perspectives in Personal Construct Theory*. London, New York: Academic Press. *116*

Shotter, J. (1973) Prolegomena to an understanding of play. *J. Theory of Behav. 3*: 47–89. *113*

Shotter, J. (1974a) The development of personal powers. In M. P. M. Richards (ed.) *The Integration of a Child into a Social World*. Cambridge: Cambridge University Press. *13, 66, 112*

Shotter, J. (1974b) What is it to be human? In N. Armistead (ed.) *Reconstructing Social Psychology*. Harmondsworth: Penguin. *44*

Skinner, B. F. (1953) *Science and Human Behaviour*. New York: Macmillan. *82*

Skinner, B. F. (1972) *Beyond Freedom and Dignity*. London: Jonathan Cape. *22, 81, 136*

Taylor, R. (1966) *Action and Purpose*. Englewood Cliffs: Prentice-Hall. *86*

Taylor, C. (1971) Interpretation and the sciences of man. *Rev. Metaphysics 25*: 3–51. *41, 119, 127*

Trevarthan, C. (2 May, 1974) Conversations with a two-month-old. *New Scientist*. *99*

Vonnegut, K. Jr. (1968) *Mother Night*. London: Jonathan Cape. *28*

Vygotsky, L. S. (1962) *Thought and Language*. Cambridge Mass.: M.I.T. Press. *21, 96*

Vygotsky, L. S. (1966) Development of the higher mental functions. In *Psychological Research in the USSR*. Moscow: Progress Publishers. *20, 21, 101*

Watson, J. B. (1913) Psychology as the behaviourist views it. *Psychological Review 20*: 158–77. *32*

Watson, J. B. (1924) *Behaviourism*. Chicago: University of Chicago Press. *45*

Weiskrantz, L. (1973) Problems and progress in physiological psychology. *Br. J. Psychol. 64*: 511–20. *47, 48, 125*

Winch, P. (1958) *The Idea of a Social Science and its Relations to Philosophy*. London: Routledge and Kegan Paul. *36, 37, 38, 86*

Wittgenstein, L. (1958) *The Blue and Brown Books*. Oxford: Blackwell. *39*

Zangwill, O. L. (1967) Psychology. In *Chambers Encyclopedia* (rev. edn). London: Pergamon Press. *46*

Subject Index